Manure Dreams
and Other Essays

Richard Holinger

Choeofpleirn Press

Copyright by Richard Holinger
2026

Choeofpleirn Press, LLC

All rights reserved.
This book may not be reproduced, in whole or in part, including illustrations, in any form for any purposes other than scholarly discussion or reviewing, without written permission from the publishers.

Although the author and publisher have made every effort to ensure that the information in this book was correct at press time, the author and publisher do not assume and hereby disclaim any liability to any party for any loss, damage, or disruption caused by errors or omissions, whether such errors or omissions result from negligence, accident, or any other cause.

Without in any way limiting the author's and publisher's exclusive rights under copyright, any use of this publication to "train" or develop generative artificial intelligence (AI) technologies is expressly prohibited.
The author and publisher reserve all rights
to license uses of this work for
generative AI training and development
of machine learning language models.

Source citations of sources were made in the original columns published by Shaw Media.

ISBN:
979-8-9991034-2-0 (print)
979-8-9991034-3-7 (digital)

Cover art by Tia Holinger, *Rock Creek Farm*

Dedication

To Tia, for her love and support in writing these essays. Also, to those who nurtured my love of creative nonfiction or helped shape these pieces into what they became: members of Night Writers Workshop (Geneva Public Library); friends Patrick Parks and Sean McCormack; colleague Alexander George (Marmion Academy); teacher Edwin Sundt (Marvelwood School); poet Donald Finkel (Washington University); writers Lore Segal and Michael Anania (The University of Illinois at Chicago).

And this book's very presence, its exquisite production, and excellent editing all derive from the good will and professional guiding hands of editors Ruth Heflin and James Cooper. Thank you for giving this book a home on Choeofpleirn's bookshelf; I could not be more honored to be part of your veteran-owned, woman-owned Kansas press that "cares about the health of the earth and our local environment."

"With a keen, observant eye, author Richard Holinger writes with deep sensitivity about the literary life, family, and the power of travel. These essays offer an honest journey into the shared human conditions of love and longing revealed through the heart of a poet."

—David W. Berner, author of the poetry collection, *Garden Tools* and the novella, *American Moon*.

Manure Dreams reclaims all the pleasures of the personal essay—a delight in scrupulously observed detail, a reflexive intelligence, deliberately self-effacing, always willing to examine its own attitudes and motivities, a delight in the unexpected weight of ordinary occasions. Holinger has a fine sense of the incongruous—the charming oddities of a small Kansas town where he taught for a year, a comic evening as the guest speaker at an Illinois Knights of Columbus literary awards dinner, boyhood summers in the title essay on a farm with the requisite animals and manure with cars from a Pullman train as its "mansion." Throughout this collection we are treated to a poet's sense of image and a fiction writer's ability to capture a character in brief bits of conversation.

—Michael Anania, author of *The Red Menace*, *In Plain Sight,* and *From the Word to the Place,* as well as *Heat Lines*, *Continuous Showings*, *Nightsongs*, *Clamors*, and *In Time*.

The profound insights in Richard Holinger's wry, appealing essays often originate in what's closest at hand—working, teaching, walking, or writing—where meaning arrives not in grand gestures but in the familiar, uncelebrated facts of daily life. Whether he's considering the foibles of his students, a charged encounter with a stranger, or his own family across generations, Holinger's journeys from observation to reflection offer gifts for him and his readers. "Each letter tapped out is a finger tracing the journey over the folds," he writes, "Until the last one leads me home." These are wise and valuable essays.

—Joe Bonomo, author of *Play This Book Loud: Noisy Essays* and *No Place I Would Rather Be: Roger Angell and a Life in Baseball Writing*

Contents

PRICKLY CONGREGATIONS

TRAVELS HERE AND THERE

IT'S COMING BACK TO ME

PRICKLY CONGREGATIONS

Manure Dreams 2

An Encounter on Brookside Pond

The windless, cloudless evening had offered up no trout. A few fish broke the surface too far from the rowboats for our beaded nymphs to reach, and those that rose nearby ignored whatever my son and I threw, even when we switched out flies every ten or fifteen minutes. The few times we got lucky, one of our wooly buggers landing in the bullseye of a round, rippling ring spreading out from a rise, the feeding trout ignored it.

"I'm heading in," Jay said, and a few minutes later, after the requisite last cast, or two, or three, behind me I heard him land and leave. I fished on, the low sun hidden by woods whose river birch, maple, aspen, tamarack, blue spruce, and white pine slowly melted together. The bald eagle, whose nest crested the Norway pine outside our cabin door, had flown over earlier, but now the small disc of sky fringed by forest, emptied of bird and cloud, forlornly sloughed off its daylight blue.

When first hearing the stomping inside the berthed rowboat, I thought Jay had reconsidered his chances, wandered back dejected but determined. Who else would arrive at dusk, less than half an hour before dark settled in? My arthritic neck allowed barely the swivel needed to catch enough of the figure's silhouette to know it wasn't Jay.

Out of patience with the fish and myself, I reeled in and rowed toward the dock to nose in for the night. Behind me, wooden oars bumped metal gunwales like pistol shots and unoiled oarlocks screeched like eaglets. Without turning, I called out, "Hope your luck's better than mine."

No response. I rowed on, now within a flyrod's flick of the dock. Hearing oars splashing farther out from the shore, I knew the other boat had launched, had to be close by. "Quiet out here," I tried again. "Not many rises."

Again, nothing. I pulled on my right oar to angle in just as the other boat's bow came in sight. A few seconds later, the boat drew alongside, and for the first time I saw the man.

This being the summer of COVID-19, I had pocketed a face mask before leaving the cabin. The thought now occurred to me to put it on, to protect this angler from any virus I had unwittingly picked up—and possibly myself from his. But because we were outdoors and separated by two or three oar lengths—and, although it should have made no difference about the decision I made, he showed no interest in covering his face—my mask stayed where it was.

He looked slightly younger than my seventy years. His round, expressionless face stared at me, the eyes unnervingly blank, the mouth unmoving, lips neither smiling nor clenched. The Aussie Slouch Hat, one side bent up to the crown, complemented his fishing vest; unlike my unwashed, haggard ruin bulging with superfluous pocket tonnage, his looked nimble and clean, glossy stainless-steel forceps hanging beside other paraphernalia in a row neat as a surgeon's tray.

We must have stayed like that, statuesque, regarding each other, for maybe five or ten seconds. Then he said my name aloud, as if it was a question.

The nickname originated with my mother reading to me when young Rudyard Kipling's story "Rikki-Tikki-Tavi." Those growing up with me would know that name. For him—whomever he was—to know it made sense.

A week before, my wife, son, and daughter had escaped Chicago's western suburb's COVID count for this club in Marinette County where I'd spent, at least in part, the last seventy summers. Many cabins on the larger Jigsaw Lake had stayed in the same family for generations; with communal dining three times a day, old acquaintances enjoyed unplanned reunions when vacations overlapped.

However, like everywhere else, the pandemic affected even this North Woods haven. Instead of gathering at our traditional tables and feeding on a bountiful buffet shoulder-to-shoulder, families entered the pinewood dining room one at a time, masked, to pick up meals boxed in plastic. Back at their cabins, family members who had no part in the pickup unloaded the plastics onto plates set on card tables that once knew only jigsaw puzzles, card games, and an occasional laptop. Screened-in porches overlooked the lake where a loon or two might paddle by, a bass splash in shallow, shadowy lily pads, or a turtle or muskrat head might surface. All the while, the mile-long lake mirrored the far bank's woods or wind might silver the surface in fish scales.

"Yeah," I confessed to the name, but couldn't come up with his. "I'm sorry, I don't remember..."

"Jim Peterson."

Ah, yes. A family of boys slightly younger than my brothers and I, which meant we met as teammates or opponents in tennis tournaments and kick the can but remained aloof as friends. Not having run into Jim at the club since we were teenagers or earlier, for all I knew he could have been a poacher come over after a couple of cold ones at the town bar.

I don't remember what I said next. Probably something inane and thoughtless like, "Oh, hi. Nice to see you again."

I clearly recall, however, what he said next. After repeating my name, he slowly added, "I remember. You were so...*cool*!"

I made a show of looking around like trying to find the person he had mistaken me for.

"You and your three brothers were *so cool*," he continued. "You scraped your chairs in the dining room."

If an adult approached our table, we were taught to stand up, a sign of respect. However, without carpeting or ceiling tiles to soak up the racket, our wooden chair legs screeched over the wooden floors, calling everyone's attention to our magnanimous gesture. "Our mother made us do that shit," I said, more an apology than explanation.

Jim reflected a moment. "I've done something all my life because of you."

My God. Where was this going? I affected another man's life-long behavior? Sure, a few students over forty years of teaching high school had shared that I turned them onto reading or writing poetry, a few even going into English education, perhaps because I raved about *Gatsby* with the gusto that math teachers reserve for favorite theorems. But I rarely hung out with Jim when we were boys and never as adults.

"All my life I've put my napkin on only one leg."

Speechless, I waited for more, waited for something to grasp, for something I could respond to. Because I had nothing to offer after fed this fact. All I could do was confirm to myself that yes, indeed, now that I thought about it, my napkin always ended up on one leg. Why? No reason. Habit. Maybe it tended to fall on the floor if bridging two legs, clung better when hung on one.

"I put it on my left leg," he detailed, "because of you."

That *is* the leg I use, I mused, never aware of it. Until now. Thanks to Jim. If pressed to answer why the left, who knew? To be scientific about it, maybe because a place setting's napkin lies on the left, under the fork, meaning one's left hand customarily frees the napkin. Descending, the napkin first encounters the left leg to land on; stopping there saves—over numerous years in one's lifetime—considerable time and energy from continuing its journey all the way over to the right, or opposite leg. Not to mention the third alternative, balancing and measuring a napkin buoyed by both legs. Admittedly, however, I'm theorizing; nothing as concrete as research or memory can be provided.

I'm sorry. I wish I had given Jim a witty reply I could record here, a laugh-aloud retort to share with you, my reader. Something like, "So, Jim, when you bring your pants to the cleaners you can tell them, 'The left leg stains aren't bad; in fact, they're all right.'"

When I did not—could not—say anything, Jim went on. "How are you?" he asked with the same expressionless face, the same politely inquiring tone. But the timing of his question threw me, something typically asked at the beginning of a conversation, not after such intimacies had been expressed.

In any case, I opened my mouth to answer with the usual, "Great," or "Fine," but before I could speak, he stopped me, as if he knew I'd not given his question the consideration he believed it deserved.

"No," he shouted, "*how* ***are*** *you*?"

That gave me pause long enough to understand he expected more than an unreflective answer. More in desperation than a mulled-over response, I returned to the topic I hadn't yet addressed. "The only way I might be cool," I began with no idea where this was going, "is being myself." I might have mentioned the epiphany in college when enlightened about a passion for writing, ever since trying to fit an hour or two in each morning, even on weekdays teaching high school. Especially those days. Imagining myself a writer exuded the confidence, autonomy, and self-esteem I never knew as a boy.

Droning on, reaching for recollections, for details, to placate Jim's query, I was saying, "Now that I'm retired, I try to..." when he cut me off again.

"No! Re*investment*."

Not sure what he meant or how to handle his correcting my vocabulary, I clambered on with my attempt to disabuse him of my "cool." "I sure didn't feel cool growing up. Perception is everything. I just wanted to be like my brothers. I *tried* to be cool. Like them. Course, that's the worst thing you can do."

He waited a beat, then proclaimed, "You *still* are cool!"

What does one say when given a compliment so undeserved? You continue to explain. "The only reason I might be 'cool' is because I've learned to be who I am, not be someone I'm not." It was the only thing that came to a feeble, stumbling mind.

Our conversation over the next ten minutes, initiated by comparing birth orders, swerved into a shared psychoanalytic session about the attention, respect, and love given, but mostly withheld, by our fathers—and how we had striven, mostly in vain, to attain those rare gifts.

Jim was the middle of five brothers, I the last of four brothers. He, in the center, had been disregarded, and I, at the end, had been infantilized.

"I was always the 'baby.' I behaved like an idiot, a clown, to get attention, to get recognized."

"Oh, yeah," Jim agreed. "My father was scarce on that. I did everything I could to get him to pay attention to me."

"It was that generation. My father told me he loved me only once." My mother was in the hospital with her first heart attack, and I had made dinner for Dad and me. I saw myself picking up our empty plates from the kitchen table when Dad said, "I love you, Tick." I said I loved him, too, mechanically, dispassionately, wishing it were truer.

I have long thought that may be the unconscious reason I write, still looking for my father's attention, still playing the fool, still wanting to be loved, still wanting to be laughed *with*.

With our paternal love/hate baggage unloaded, we parted. We both promised to write, each knowing neither one would. We said our goodbyes. I rowed the boat in and wrapped the anchor line around the base of a tree. Before walking back to the cabin, I listened for a rustling that might suggest the yearling bear who earlier that week we had watched scamper through prickly, dense undergrowth and scratch his way up a nearby tree. Hearing nothing but the night's first whip-poor-will, that cheery but lonely command sending me back to boyhood's bedtime while sunset's orange light filtered through drawn shades, I picked up my flyrod and net and started home.

Walking back, I thought about how quickly and profoundly I'd been thrust into this intimate stranger's life. How unnerved I became when hearing his life-long feelings and habits that added up, really, to nothing more than a younger kid looking up to an older kid's misperceived cool—and a napkin's left thigh placement! Was it the simple honesty of nostalgia that brought out Jim's forthright, naked truths and eccentric questioning? Or the friendly encouragement of one or two cocktails before and, perhaps, after dinner? Or just the need, the urge, to deliver his truest musings to someone in the rowboat next to his, someone like him out to throw a few flies after dinner, someone who figured more as a memory than as a person, a young boy's funhouse mirror image blurred and distorted by time and circumstance?

Bringing back no fish through woods now nearly dark, I hauled instead a stringer of moods and remembrances. I don't know why, but they weighed on me more than any number of trout that might have been pulled from Brookside Pond's deep, dark, cold holes. Pulled them in through nervous fingers, then feeding out line and letting them run, until, feeling them tire, drawing them back, never not aware of their

fright, their anger, their resistance to the catch,
and all the while fearing they might get away.

K of C

The stone building looks impermeable to irony. At the entrance to the parking lot, a poster the size of a tollway exit sign warns:

Abortion:
America's #1
Killer

"What time is it?" my wife asks. She has consented to come along, but would rather be anywhere else, as would I.

"5:27:46." Precision is easy with a digital watch. "They told me cocktails at 5:30. Want to drive around?"

Twice I turn south down northbound one-way streets. Tia suggests I might be bottlenecking some anxiety. "Want me to drive?" she says, insinuating incompetency.

I stop far beyond an intersection's white wait line. A turning car comes close to scraping our grill. "Where do you want to go?" I ask.

"Back."

We've reached the main drag of Aurora, Illinois, one of those Midwestern towns that decades ago fell into disrepair and is now trying to reinvent itself. The February sunset, instead of glazing everything with a golden hue, spotlights pockmarked brick storefronts, a tired theater, and pegleg parking meters. We follow railroad tracks that artery outward from downtown's heart, passing auto body shops and a building advertising sharpening services. On the valley's slight rise above the Fox River, rows of large, decaying houses resemble dull, brown mausoleums. Eight minutes later we're back in the parking lot.

"K of C." Tia points out the towering black letters hung on the building's side.

"Knights of Columbus," I say.

"Kentucky Fried Chicken," she suggests.

I know only a little about the organization, Catholic men (no women) who do something good for society. The division heads are "Supreme" leaders: Supreme Knight, Supreme Chaplain, Deputy Supreme Knight, Supreme Secretary, Supreme Treasurer, and so on. Given their talent for monikers suggesting ability and hierarchy, I'm surprised the Deputy Supreme Knight is not called "Less Than" or "Lower Than" Supreme Knight.

Writing about this now, from my vantage point in the third decade of the 21st century, this all-male society reminds me of a dinosaur unaware of the meteor flaming down. However, in the early 1980s, especially within the conservative, patriarchal Catholic zeitgeist, organizations like this did not flinch. In fact, they prospered and grew, the last bastion against, well, everything not to their liking.

The three parked cars look like they've been dropped off for parts. "Doesn't look like many people here yet," I say.

"It's kind of tacky," Tia lets me know, "for the guest speaker to sit in a parked car in sub-freezing temperatures."

We enter a dark brown side door. Following directions received from the teaching colleague who got me into this, we take an immediate right, down narrow linoleum stairs edged with aluminum stripping. In the basement, plastic wood paneling and speckled indoor-outdoor carpeting absorb most of the 60-watt lighting in what might be a reception room. The room to our left is unlit, so perhaps off limits. The room to our right sheds a dim, golden, sunset light. That leaves the room loaded with tables.

"Are you sure women are invited?" Tia asks, but I'm too busy questioning *my* invitation to worry about hers. The colleague who asked me to write up something and deliver it tonight asked because I was an English teacher and sometime writer; tonight's ceremony is to celebrate middle school essay winners.

I take Tia's coat into a small cloakroom where two racks of wire hangers dangle nakedly. I think about announcing our arrival by swinging the first metal hanger into the second to domino a skeletal chime, a spontaneous Harry Bertoia sound sculpture.

I rejoin Tia and walk into the lighted room where two men in black tuxedoes huddle near a podium between two long tables. They remind me of Alec Guinness and Peter Ustinov plotting a bank robbery. When we catch one's attention, he takes small, calculated Captain, May I? steps toward us. A flashy red, white, and blue sash cuts diagonally across his chest.

"I bet I know who you are!" he shouts at me from ten feet away. "Robert!"

"No," I say, sorry to disappoint his robust welcome.

"Bob!" he tries again.

"No."

"Rob?"

"Richard," I say. "Rick."

"And you are his charming wife," he tells Tia, then adds, "Robert, a martini!" Whether he demands it or offers me one I'm uncertain, but he uses the drink to lure us into the sunset-lit room that turns out to be a bar. Our host introduces us to the bartender and then, before disappearing, says, "Just mention your school, and they'll get you anything you like."

The bartender, a 50-something man, wears a simple, white, button-down Oxford. Tia and I sit at a table where people pass on the news that tonight's awards' recipients are not high school students—as I had thought—but eighth graders. I consider the Grand Canyon separating an audience of 13- and 18-year-olds, but even if I wanted to revise my speech, the dusky light and my stressed-out, panicked nerves prevent it. The three imitation gas lamps hanging on the faux veneer would never let me revise more than the title. Next, I'm told the theme of the essay contest, "What being an American means to me," should be reflected in the guest speaker's addresses. Instead, my speech, "The good news and bad news about being a writer," mentions nothing about being an American, only a writer.

The host returns to introduce us to the first guests under 60-years-old, an Assistant Superintendent and a teacher at Mooseheart Child City and School, respectively.

"We are run by the Order of the Moose," the Assistant Superintendent tells us. "We are a self-contained city. We are a living and educational environment for parentless children. We have children from eight months to 19-years-old. We have a full sports program. Of course, we aren't very competitive because we're so small. We started taking children of divorced parents in 1973."

His description lasts half an hour of head nodding until the Super's wife breaks in to describe her lymph node operation. As soon as she's described being sewn up, the teacher, who quit smoking in 1978, starts giving away a carton of Kools.

Our host rounds us up for dinner. Each place setting on the gold-speckled white Formica tabletops consists of a blue plastic knife and fork on either side of a paper mat showing off a black-and-white drawing of the chunky K of C building. The dining room decor saps an appetite: off-white tile flooring; plastic paneling except behind the podium where someone stuck a twelve-foot wall resembling an English Tudor exterior; flags sandwiching the lectern—on one side American, the other, a highly-colorful local drape, either the City of Aurora or the K of C banner. On the lectern, a yellow plaque instructs, "PLEASE WAIT TO BE SEATED."

We are not at the head table, nearest the lectern. Rather, our table is one of many circled around the room, the arrangement resembling a spinning teacup carnival ride. Once everyone is seated and quiet, our host, the sashed emcee, welcomes the room, then calls up a Catholic brother, a large African American man wearing a black suit, white collar, and Buddy Holly glasses. He mumbles a blessing on food nowhere in sight. When he sits down, the emcee announces, "We're going to the buffet in a very democratic fashion: head table first, then tables to my left, center, and so forth."

The food is brought in in deep rectangular tinfoil trays and lined up on empty breakdown tables. When directed, our group stands and waits in line behind four other tables already waiting. I notice nailed to the entrance of the aforementioned mysteriously unlit room a carved "KNIGHTS" sign under which a red arrow points, I'm pretty sure, toward the MEN'S room.

"Excuse me," I announce to anyone in line who cares. A few strangers nod or look questioningly at my departure. Into the cave I stroll, a jaunty knight parrying tables and chairs but finding no hint of a porcelain Grail with flush mechanism. I backtrack to the reception room and decide the only remaining unexplored portal leads to the coat room where, by going through a yellow-tiled hallway reminiscent of subway tunnels, I finally find the KNIGHTS' room.

Here expense was not spared. Here the building's original romantic aspirations look fulfilled. Urinals stretch tall as coffins; toilet bowls serpentine; sinks bottom out wide and deep as baptismal fonts. Here is the historical K of C story, over time gone to rust, literally and figuratively, by inflation, taxes, and decreasing piety. This vault bears a truth; spared of false facades, this bathroom feels honest as a bomb shelter. In here, I feel safe. Even the toilet paper looks sincere: yellow, cracked, and wrinkled as the *Constitution*'s parchment.

Back in the chow line, I load up my plate along with my tablemates who have finally made it to the food. The servers, clones of the bartender, say devilish things to the ladies like, "With your figure, you can afford *two* pieces of beef!" The roast beef is pre-sliced thin as oak leaves and looks dark and dry as bark. Prongs drop two pieces into the entree section of my cardboard plate, then the other two squares fill with powdered potatoes and canned, olive-green green beans. Over everything a blessing of gluey, brown gravy is poured. Because I'm out of plate pockets, a roll the size of a Rubik's Cube, a pad of butter sandwiched with paper, and a rectangular lemon square plop atop the ubiquitous gravy. Another table offers Styrofoam cups of steaming, pre-poured coffee.

For the next forty-five minutes, until the emcee calls for our attention, the Mooseheart folks feed us information about their city and school. I barely listen, knowing I'll soon be addressing an audience of middle schoolers who wrote about the meaning of what is it to be an American, expecting me to follow suit. I am about to disappoint them with a speech about being a writer.

The emcee first introduces the K of C's Fifth Warden whom, he jokes, was just released from Joliet prison. Ha! Big response. A man wearing a sports jacket as orange as a bonfire grips the podium, tells us he's just had his joke stolen, then proceeds to tell it again, changing the names and location, but keeping the same punchline. He follows that up with five serious minutes of patriotic rhetoric, employing words like pride, ambition, sacrifice, and courage, all delivered better than an Armed Forces recruiting officer. It's a speech he's given countless times before because it addresses emotions, not intellect, the platitudes delivered with such pharisaic ebullience I'm positive he'll soon be promoted to First Warden.

Next, the emcee points to a gray-haired lady at one of the two head tables. She was married to a K of C member, now deceased, and is being honored for, from what I gather, having married him. She rises, with difficulty, to thank everyone for remembering her husband this way. As she sits, applause inflates the room, though I guarantee only a few of us could pick the dead man out of a lineup of two.

When introduced, I stand and deliver my speech, the one written for high school students, of which there are none present. I'm a mime for the blind, a storyteller for the deaf. The writers keep waiting for me to tell them what it's like being an American, keep looking up at me as though because I'm the guest speaker I have a lock on what an essay on the topic should sound like. Instead, they hear about the writer's creative process, the writer's passion. Of course, eighth graders have homework to do, assignments to write, not manuscripts to finish, so my efforts to engage them in the artistic emotions of professional writers falls flat. From the look on everyone's faces, or those who look awake, I get the feeling they'd rather have the Fifth Warden back for an encore.

Once I'm out of the way, the emcee gets down to business. "Now we come to the part of the program we've all been waiting for—the presentation of awards for the nine best essays on 'What Being an American Means to Me.' Before announcing the winners, I will read a passage from a famous American, then read just one paragraph from each prize-winning essay until we get to the first-place essay. That will be read in its entirety because it deserves to be read all the way through."

He pauses. Has he misplaced a page? Have his patent leather shoes clouded? No. He looks confident. He waits, as we do, for the next move.

Suddenly, the two tuxedoed men with whom the emcee had earlier planned the bank robbery appear in the dining room entrance. Each sports a hat and epaulets like a 19th century British naval officer. They carry on their belts a three-foot sheathed sword whose chain jingles as they walk. They do not smile. This is not Halloween, nor is it entertainment. This is ritual, meant to impress, to inspire, to convey a tone of solemnity. This is the Fourth Estate (a red, white, and blue pamphlet on our table informs us), a group of select K of C members who pass rigorous standards: 1) Be a veteran, 2) Be 21-years-old or older, 3) Be a practicing Catholic, and 4) Believe in America.

Their mission? Promote patriotism.

They round the podium on their march to the head table where a third Fourth Estater (the emcee being the fourth) stands. I soon find out this third Fourth will dole out the awards: ninth- through fourth-place essays receive certificates suitable for framing; third- through first-place essays are handed checks of $25, $50, and $100 respectively. I wonder how eighth graders will spend their money: blow it on a cache of Double Bubble, retire early from middle school, or, acceding to mommy and daddy's insistence, stash it in the bank to earn interest.

The swashbuckling Fourth Estaters slice through a series of movements as though spelling out "How stupid do I look?" Their heraldry finished, they rest their dull sword points on the tile floor. The emcee then revs up his voice and launches into the first sentence of the *Declaration of Independence* followed by, "And now, from the ninth-place winner's essay...."

Holding up a piece of onionskin paper, he races through monosyllabic diction that, although reflecting a parent's ideology, sounds surprisingly clean and detailed as if proofed by an English teacher. When the paragraph ends, a name is announced and a chubby, bespectacled boy in a navy wool pullover approaches from an orbiting table, embarrassed to be the ninth-place winner in a field of nine winning essayists.

While winding his way to the podium, he sees the Fourth Estaters snap to attention, cross and recross their weapons, then raise their blades up to their faces, nose-hair close. We catch on: the winner is meant to pass between these aging Zorros. The boy, however, has not been told the game plan, and after witnessing these sabre-waving suburban matadors, he goes around the podium, circumventing the enemy. The Fifth Warden saves the day by directing the coward back the way he came and sending him through the Fourth Estates' tuxedoed Colossi of Rhodes.

The expectations for accepting awards now clear, the emcee maniacally reads a paragraph from each of the eighth to second place papers. We hear what it's like to be American by alluding to Francis Scott Key, Ralph Waldo Emerson, Abraham Lincoln, and other iconic figures. When finally reaching the first-place essay, he downshifts for emphasis. This is the big moment, the big reveal, not so much to announce the winner (there is only one student left without an award), but to parade the creativity and brilliance that a hundred-dollar essay affords.

He begins to read, slowly this time. We hear about a Vietnamese girl's flight from her country. Her family arranges a night escape by boat, but in the confusion of getting to the pickup site, the girl and her mother are separated from her father and two brothers. They must decide whether to leave their land, their country, their home, as planned, or stay and try to unite—not knowing, of course, what the others will do, can do. Feeling helpless but undaunted, they stick with their plan.

They eventually land in San Francisco where they share with many others a two-room apartment. For a year and a half, they search and wait for their missing family members. The memoir ends with their family's reunification, a metaphor for Vietnam itself.

Having seen *The Killing Fields* a week before, I blink back tears. The essay's style is jerky, but honest. She has delivered excruciating loss, raw fear, and joyful thanksgivings. Her real-life story entrances, horrifies. The other essays have gushed over America and its by now trite, overused, meaningless "land of the free" and "home of the brave" phrases. The other writers' work was fueled by hollow, abstract nouns and dull, collective references to once heroic figures. We got baseball gloves and Girl Scout cookies.

The judge picked wisely, choosing the most original submission. It told not only America's truth, but the writer's truth. And she wrote it in English, her second language, learned in her second land.

Everyone stands to applaud. A camera's light flashes as she receives her congratulations and the cash envelope. The clapping continues as she walks back to her table. We are now applauding her family. We are applauding survival. We are applauding their coming to America in spite of the U.S. bombing her country and her fellow Vietnamese people. We are applauding our own ancestors, those immigrants who made a similar trip and who took a similar chance. We are applauding First Place.

Things die down. My guess, my hope, is that Tia and I will be on our way home in just a few minutes.

Not so. The emcee introduces a priest, the principal of the winning essayist's school. He says things like, "I'd like to thank the Knights for sponsoring this essay competition," and, "I'd like to encourage the boys and girls here tonight to pursue their excellence in writing."

I'm certain that's the end until the emcee calls on the religious brother to deliver the benediction. He and his stomach hang over the podium.

"Before I get...to the benediction...." His sentence stretches out longer than the melted cheese on the first bite of hot pizza. "...I'd like to take a few...of your precious moments to say...a few words about a very...worthwhile cause. Now I don't mean to be derogatory, but the...wives of lots of the men here tonight...before they go out to a...party or...meeting, sometimes need a...facelift."

Tables around me gasp, titter, and chuckle in between undercurrents of hushed retorts.

"Well, our Statue of Liberty...is having one."

The rest of his call to action is trampled by women's outrage. Even the head table's elderly widow looks miffed, telling her Fourth Estate dinner partner a thing or two I wish I could hear. I can only imagine the holy brother has no wife and very few women friends.

"And finally," he continues, the room quieting with the promise of a subject change, "I would like to thank all of you...who wrote essays for this...uh,...this..."

"Contest," the Fifth Warden coaches.

"Contest, yes. And thank you for your...uh...donations, sort of, to the...contest." By the time he calls on the Father, Son, and Holy Spirit, the crowd has turned on him; even the Triumvirate cannot save him. However, just as Crusading knights were afforded a prayerful sendoff, so do we deserve and receive one tonight.

When the emcee re-establishes himself at the lectern, he thanks the brother, the Fifth Warden, the widow, the guest speaker, the Fourth Estaters, the essayists, the principal, and everyone else for coming. Then, finally, he wishes us all, "Goodnight!"

Leaving the dining room, we see the emcee, like a pastor after his service, shaking hands and chatting briefly with his flock. When our turn comes, he cranks my hand as we both fabricate lies.

"This really has been a delightful evening," I say.

"You gave a wonderful speech."

"Thank you so much for the delicious dinner."

"I appreciate your donating your valuable time."

"I really enjoyed talking to the people from Mooseheart."

"We couldn't have had a better speaker."

Leaving Tia for a few moments, I squeeze by people crowding the coatroom. After grabbing both our coats, I notice a blond-haired boy, a fifth or sixth place winner, who looks as though he has just been told, "No video games for a week, young man." Seeing his dour expression, his parents try to comfort him in low, encouraging tones.

After they finish trying to buoy him up, I pass by. "I think you should have won," I whisper, just in case the Vietnamese family might be nearby. "I really liked the part about...," I begin, reciting his words back to him as closely as I can remember them. It is the greatest compliment I can think of giving this writer, letting him know that I listened to, and remembered, what he wrote.

I don't think it helps, but the parents smile anyway. Maybe sixth place will make him a better writer, in the long run, than coming in first.

If ever asked back, I'll be sure to put that in my speech.

What This World Needs Is More "Sitting 'til Bedtime"

Reading Wendell Berry this morning made me feel guilty I wasn't doing more for my community, my state, my world.

If you're wondering, "Who's this Berry guy?", the back cover of *The World-Ending Fire: The Essential Wendell Berry* describes him as "an essayist, novelist, and poet." Obama awarded him the National Humanities Medal.

But most important, surely, to him, he is still (at the time of this writing) a farmer and husband in Henry County, Kentucky and cares about how we care for the world. According to Dean Kuipers, "...Berry is a prophet of the domestic. These essays are about how to make a household here on earth."

He also writes about talk. In "The Work of Local Culture," a friend recalls, "There used to be a sort of institution in our part of the country known as 'sitting till [sic] bedtime.' After supper,...neighbors would walk across the fields to visit each other. They popped corn,...ate apples and talked. They told each other stories.... When bedtime came, the visitors lit their lanterns and went home.... They had everything but money."

Berry reflects, "They were poor,...but they had each other's comfort when they needed it, and they had their stories, their history together in that place. To have everything but money is to have much. And most people of the present can only marvel to think of neighbors entertaining themselves for a whole evening without a single imported pleasure."

It's no surprise that *Health Day* reports, "Half of young Americans between the ages of 12 and 17 spend at least four hours each day on their smartphones, computers or televisions."

Does that let parents and grandparents off the hook? Hardly. The more we rely on our phones, laptops, and TVs to escape ourselves, our loneliness, the sooner we die.

Take it from Harvard University: "[S]ocializing is tied to reduced risks of early death." In one study, "the more people socialized, the longer they lived. Each of the following groups lived longer than the one before it: those who socialized occasionally, monthly, weekly, or every day. People in any of these groups lived longer than those who did not socialize at all."

Even though I've got a "stable of doctors" (as my brother calls it), and a trough full of prescription meds, I've taken to the road to meet people. Sometimes, "It don't come easy," as Ringo Starr sang years ago, for an introverted writer like me, but I've seen the writing on the tomb wall.

There are plenty of groups to discover at libraries and bookstores—or start your own, say, breakfast club. In fact, my wife, Tia, along with a few friends, formed their own book discussion group.

Well, that's not entirely accurate. They choose a book to read, meet at each other's houses for dinner, and talk a lot. If mention of the book's title came up by chance over the tiramisu, well, fine for five, ten minutes, then back to, "I'll have another splash of cab, please, and what's Maggie doing after Brown?"

Or reach out to friends not seen for a while. Recently, I called my old boarding school roommate, now living in Nevada.

"Hi, Rick. I'm just eating my oatmeal at the Senior Center. We have sixteen cakes donated for the raffle today. I went to look at them. Sixteen, can you believe it?"

Sure, I can. Most people are kind.

Gotta go. I'm finishing Bob Newhart's memoir for a "Humor" book discussion group at the St. Charles library. Seriously! Instead of aspirin, I'll take two chapters and call a friend in the morning.

Arguing *The Scarlet Letter*'s Demise

I'll be the first to admit my mistake. From page one, my students needed more guidance to make their way unscathed through the famous novel. I sent them off on their own, however, with only study questions to lead them through the great briar patch of Romantic symbolism. Although most of them survived, they came out on the other side bleeding and angry.

Because this essay is, in a way, a story at heart, allow me to describe the setting and characters. Geographically, our school sits an hour west of Chicago surrounded by suburbs. To our single-sex parochial school offering JROTC, students generally come from Catholic families, carry respectful—and sometimes impressive—GPAs, and often brag an alumni legacy. Specifically, the class in question, English 3 Honors, includes most of the top-ranked students in the junior class. That didn't mean, however, as I learned soon enough, they could wrestle their Proteus to a standstill without help from an Athena.

Soon after delivering the assignment to read chapters one through five in Nathaniel Hawthorne's *Scarlet Letter* and respond to study questions, I heard hostility whenever the novel's title or author came up. Over two months, resentment grew into a boil that had to be lanced; had I asked them instead to copy word for word the entire text of *Moby Dick*, they would gladly have chosen it over plowing again through Dimmesdale's guilt, Hester's shame, Chillingworth's revenge, and Pearl's dialogue, celebrating every turn of the pen.

Therefore, I let them vent. Their essay question on the first semester exam went something like this: "Many of you argued vociferously that you did not like Hawthorne's novel; a few admired it grudgingly. Prove to me the novel's failing—or its success—as a great work of American literature."

I never saw students race through objective questions so fearlessly in order to help me understand the book's shortcomings. Dimmesdale's misery, Hester's ignominy, Chillingworth's vindictiveness, and Pearl's tantrums paled in comparison to their feelings at having to spend hours fighting their way through the labyrinthine prose. Undoubtedly, a roomful of young females would have responded much the same.

The boys ravaged nearly every aspect of the book except its cover art, beginning with the drawn-out descriptions. "The over-inflated story could be compared to a walk in the park," Nick suggested. "Instead of simply walking through the park, every blade of grass is described."

Karl expressed his frustration with the author's style. "The wordiness of every sentence confuses and puts the reader into an angry frenzy because of the inability to dissect a page-long sentence with outdated, ornate words."

Michael R. offered a psychological analysis. "This novel is self-destructive for teenage readers. My thesis epitomizes what it takes to read the book, and that is literary conditioning."

Brian encapsulated many of Hawthorne's weaknesses in his critique. "Hawthorne took an intriguing storyline chock full of the necessary ingredients to make it into an exciting read (Sins! Deception! Out-of-wedlock sexual affairs, Oh my!) and sucked every last drop of interest out of it. 'How did he perform such a feat?' you ask. By his verbose use of dialogue (look at me! I'm using 'VERBOSE' just thinking about it!), there is a fine line between beautiful description and absolute wordiness, and Hawthorne crossed it immediately after the first line."

Eddie set his sights on the dialogue: "When the little girls speak to each other saying how they will throw mud at Hester and Pearl, it is just ridiculous. No girl today would say, 'Come hither and let us fling mud upon them.'"

As wordy and archaic as they thought the prose, another aspect of style frustrated them even more. Brett complained, "Like most Romantic writers, Hawthorne takes symbolism and beats the reader over the head with it. There is no need to search for a hidden meaning behind a character or object; it is spelled out."

Charlie offered, "The ethereal A in the sky added nothing other to heighten the feeling of ridiculousness."

All this description naturally leads to plot block. Michael R. asserted the plot "Moves as fast as a tortoise pulling a Boeing 747 on a rope. Edgar Allan Poe's plot in *The Fall of the House of Usher* keeps the reader feeling he is covering ground, whereas in *The Scarlet Letter*, you can read for an hour, and in the book, five minutes have gone by." Eric concurred: "You can only talk about adultery so much before you beat it into the ground, but Hawthorne managed to tack on another fifty pages."

As for excitement, "One of the scarce bits of action," Michael M. found, "was Hester on the platform in the beginning, and even that is pushing it." Peter described the slow pacing as "A death of action in the text. Books like *The DaVinci Code* sell out because of an action-packed plot. Hester trying to raise Pearl, cope with Puritan society, and deal with Chillingworth lacks the fast-paced action of car chase scenes that modern audiences want."

Sam resorted to Latinate terms: "This book uses *in medias res* in a bad way. The story of Hester's affair with Dimmesdale would have been much more interesting than its aftermath. The book starts in true falling action of a normal story, but it still manages to drag on for a couple hundred pages."

"I expected a duel between Chillingworth and Dimmesdale," confided Bennett, "and what happens? Dimmesdale confesses, then dies for no apparent reason. Hawthorne could have intrigued the reader but instead gives a morality check."

A few students gave the book, if not a positive review, a grudging acceptance, Anthony acquiescing that it "was not pure evil," and Cory pointing out the "accurate depiction of the period. The Puritan timeframe was not one of car crashes and bomb explosions. It was a time of contemplation. Our society needs to look at different times to see how different we have become." Sam admired the novel, "as a character study; like the movie *Jarhead*, you felt like you know the characters even though nothing happens to them."

As Pudd'nhead, Wilson might have said, "Taken all around," even for the students who claimed to respect one or two aspects of the book, its dirge-like prose failed to rock these teenagers. "Our modern time affects how we view this story," argued Nick. "We live in a 'go-go' society where if a movie does not have what we want, we change the channel."

"This story is not relevant to our time," Michael M. argued. "People don't get forced to wear letters on their clothes or get exiled from town, or at least not that much. If reading this book wasn't majorly affecting my grade, I would have tossed it aside after the first chapter."

So, to paraphrase F. Scott Fitzgerald, this has been a story of the teacher after all. I should have suggested earlier that the demerits posted on the bulletin board in the school's main hallway bear a resemblance to Hester's public humiliation; that the burka worn by Middle Eastern women suggest second-class citizenship; that not farther than four desks away from any student probably sits someone who feels as displaced from the school's soul as Hester lived from the town's center; that no matter how great your fame or talent, you can always do something to anger others and find yourself targeted for exclusion and death, as Salman Rushdie well knows.

I haven't yet made up my mind whether to keep *The Scarlet Letter* on next year's reading list. Maybe I should listen to the rising voices of anger and angst. After all, it's just one book among many available. Substituting Arthur Miller's *The Crucible* would work as well. Besides, I'm reminded of Jeff Daniel's character in the film *The Squid and the Whale*, a college professor and washed-up novelist who, when hearing his son had to read *A Tale of Two Cities*, declares it, "Minor Dickens," then complains along the lines of, "Why do high school teachers always pick the worst books by the greatest writers?"

My first English graduate school course was "Hawthorne." We read every novel and story he wrote. Even then the stories drew me in more than the novels, the short works brimming with edgy characters, quirky plots, and supernatural trimmings. The longer works, as rich and ornamental as Hester's letter, simply put, belabored what soon became obvious. If that sounds as reductive as my students' essays, well, count me in with their numbers; they've got a point.

What's the real reason our curriculum included Hawthorne's masterpiece? We are a college preparatory school, and the notion that colleges expect our students to be versed in the canon has survived the era of postmodern deconstruction. As much as one would like to scoff at the tradition and declare it outdated as Shirley Jackson's anachronistic lottery held in the town that never grew up, the sacred list, at least for now, needs its congregation's attention.

Maybe, however, I could compromise. After giving it five minutes' thought, I came up with a plan. I would drop the turgid Hawthorne and pick up the turgid Melville. After forcing my students to read *Moby Dick* outside of class, with only study questions to guide their way, not through the dark woods of Puritanical theocracy and hypocrisy, but through the self-destructive, insane obsessions of hunt and destroy, I'll give them the same first semester exam question into which a new title has been inserted.

The following year, it'll be *The Sound and the Fury*; the year after that, *The Golden Bowl* or

Ethan Frome. Maybe *O Pioneers* would speak to them. Or *Their Eyes Were Watching God*. Or *School Days of an Indian Girl.*

With so many great American novels at my dispersal and disposal, I would retire before running out of juicy, ripe lemons to squeeze annually into literary lemonade. Though my students may not have appreciated Hawthorne's luxurious syntax or his favorite theme, the "magnetic chain of humanity," they learned about writing honestly in a voice all their own.

That's worth a hundred car chases and *DaVinci Codes.*

Epiphany

I hear the Ford's 9-passenger truck before Matt turns into the driveway and parks by the detached garage. On this murky, foggy morning, as he and his two boys unload, Matt takes off his wool cap and perches his sunglasses above his forehead. A graying Burl Ives beard suggests an early middle age. He wears an unzipped sweatshirt, blue jeans, and lace-up boots. Evan, the elder boy, and Less, the younger, ten and five respectively, from different marriages, belong to Matt for the weekend. All three gather on the couch in our living room.

Across the room by a gas fireplace humming flames, sits my son Jack, thirty-three, in a padded armchair. My wife, Tia, sits in the twin blue chair beside him. I sit on a long, lidded bench lined with a soft gray material, my back up against a picture window overlooking a grass-mown hill flowing down to Lake Campton.

Matt works for Jack, a landscape architect, who started his own business several years ago after working for several large, impersonal, cutthroat, Chicago landscaping conglomerations. In good capitalistic tradition, his clientele has expanded and with it his equipment, including two trucks, three trailers, a reticulated Bobcat, rider mower, self-propelled push mower, two snowblowers (one gas, one electric), a woodchipper, a wood splitter, a stump grinder, and assorted electric and gas-powered saws, drills, leaf blowers, welders, etc.

Before Jack sits down, he hands Evan and Less each a Christmas-themed shopping bag (with handles) as large as checked-through luggage, then sets down Matt's bag, smaller, though apparently heavier from the way it *clunk*s onto the coffee table. Each boy pulls a giftwrapped box from the bag and struggles with the ribbon. Jack finds a pair of scissors in the kitchen drawer and snips where needed. Tearing off the snowflake blizzard paper, they find identical gray plastic drones.

"One for each," Jack says, "so they can have aerial fights."

Evan takes his out of the box and begins piecing it together as Less unwraps a tube of colored pencils. Because he looks lost and bored, I find a piece of old stationery in my desk and give it to him so he can start drawing.

Meanwhile, Jack has begun to help Evan manipulate screws smaller than those attaching a temple to eyeglasses. Matt pulls out of his gift bag the first thing he sees, something that looks like a heavy, pewter LP record with clock hands spearing out from its center.

"What is it?" I ask.

"It's the sawblade," Jack says, "we used to cut bricks and pavers this year to fit hardscape walks and patios."

"Oh, that's cool, man." Jack stares, smiling, at the blade, turning it over and fingering the timepiece's mechanism and twirling the minute and hour hands.

"The clock part needs a little work."

"Sure."

Jack and Evan fit batteries into the drone's control box and red and blue lights blink on and off beneath and on top of the propellered wings.

"My favorite colors," says Less, looking up from his drawing. "Blue and red."

"You have trees where you're going to live?" I ask Matt.

Currently, Matt lives with his ex-wife, but soon will be renting an apartment over a stable housing horses and who knows how many cats.

"Sure," Matt smiles. "Lots. But not around the barn."

"Drones like trees as much as kites," I say. "Jack's first drone, not even his, his aunt's, blew into a Norway pine sixty feet up. He was trying to film a nest of bald eagles, and the wind took the drone into the branches."

Jack unwraps the gift Matt has brought him, a bottle of Woodford Reserve. He offers to open and share a sample, even though it's only 9:45 A.M.

"Sure," Matt says and smiles.

Beyond the picture window as large as "Night Watch," a white fog clouds the lake, only small islands of pale winter grass visible among slowly melting snow. Jack pours a couple of ounces of the dark alcohol into two highball glasses and drops into each a circular ice cube. They click glasses and toast the season. Neither is a believer, but they have faith in the spirit this time of year brings.

Evan continues to construct his drone with Jack's help. Less chooses an olive-green pencil and draws the outline of an off-balanced heart then fills it with a purple pencil. Blood?

"What's that?" I ask.

Less looks up, not at me, but straight ahead, at nothing discernable. His eyes widen, his mouth opens wide, but he makes no sound.

Matt looks down at his son beside him. "Have an epiphany?"

For a moment, Less says nothing. Then, slowly turning his head toward his father, says, "No. But I had an idea."

A beat, then we all laugh—except for Less, who looks pleased with himself, with us, with our laughter.

I remember the poem I started to write but couldn't get beyond the first couple of lines. Titled, "God's Dilemma," the poem seemed, up until this moment, to have stalled.

Then, suddenly, just like that, the rest of it comes to me.

Good Graces

ONE: The Review

Two months before COVID forced everyone inside, I published a volume of poetry, *North of Crivitz*. The pieces, formal and free verse, featured Northwoods, rural, and small-town settings. The book sold like most first books of poetry written by an unknown—badly. I doubt more than 200 books were sold.

Months later, on Amazon, I saw a lone one-star review:

> *E. Lewis*
> ★☆☆☆☆ ***Remember Dave Etter***
> *Reviewed in the United States on February 12, 2021*
>
> *I dislike that this hack passes himself as a poet and a [sic] attempts to work himself into the good graces of real poets. He had no respect for other poets and recently sold inscribed books by Dave Etter, who considered him a friend.*

Stunned. Horrified. Shocked. Confused. Who excoriated me as a poet and person? Who knew about selling my books and would lambaste me as a traitor? What did my book's worth have to do with Dave, an award-winning Illinois poet I knew as a friend?

I shared the review with friend and novelist, Patrick Parks, who advised me to write Amazon and have it deleted as hate speech. "It's not a review," he said. "It's an attack."

I filled out Amazon's complaint form then searched the internet for E. Lewis, even though believing both actions a waste of time. More than a year later, the review stands; read it for yourself.

I did, however, find E. Lewis.

TWO: The Books

Books, literally, lined the walls. Wallpapered them. Three to four thousand. Our cheap, built-in bookcases ran the length of two walls. Most books I bought in my twenties and thirties, when used bookstores were my Ithaca. I collected college and grad school assigned and unassigned texts and books recommended by teachers and friends. Most were first editions, many signed.

When my son bought a house, my wife and I decided to sell ours and live with him. The books needed to be moved or sold. Libraries were no longer the go-to drop-off place for pre-read books. There was limited storage space at the new house. My son only wanted my fly fishing books, and my daughter wanted only the limited edition, signed *Leaves of Grass*.

I faced a Sophie's Choice. Books inscribed by poets Dave Etter (for whom I had written many reviews and essays when he published these books), no one in my family wanted.

Even if I could find bookshelf space, to what end? To bookend on a mantel or living room sideboard to impress the unimpressible visitor who never heard of Dave? To impress literary friends who might then be envious or derogatory? To collect dust?

Unlike Sophie giving up half her beloveds, I gave up virtually all of mine.

THREE: The Pickup

Because the collection included some truly valuable items, I queried antiquarian and rare booksellers. A bookseller from Uncharted Books came out from Chicago who, after three or four hours, had three or four neat stacks on the floor and named a price. "I can go over each book if you want," he said.

"Not necessary."

"Are you sure you're okay with that?" he asked, meaning the figure he'd given me.

He was paying me to take books out of the house, and if I couldn't trust an antiquarian and rare book dealer supposedly in love with books, who could I trust?

When he left, I couldn't tell that any books had been removed.

"Are you sad?" my wife asked, "at seeing your books go?"

Yes, the loss felt like a death in the family.

FOUR: Dave

To get to his house in the 1980s and 90s, I travel fifteen minutes west to on Route 38, a two-lane highway leading eventually to Dekalb, turn off Elburn's Main Street and take a couple rights.

Dave Etter sits on the front porch of his two-story white house looking comfortable and kickback. He holds a pipe in one hand, a cup of coffee or a glass of beer, depending on the time of day, in the other. I park on the street's grassy shoulder and walk under the tall, full, green trees to meet him. He delivers a witty welcome then puts out his hand and says in his low, gravelly voice, "Thanks for comin' out," like I'd crossed the state to get there. He gives me that half-smile beneath a scraggly Mark Twain mustache, eyes twinkling behind thick-framed glasses. Dave is balding and has the paunch that doctors annually warn against, suggesting exercise and diet.

Occasionally my wife and I are invited to join Dave and his wife Peggy, along with son George and daughter Emily, for dinner in their Victorian dining room. However, I preferred days Dave asks me to come over by myself, when he and I dive into poetry and listen to his favorite jazz musicians (Thelonious Monk more often than not) on his record player in the small, cramped library packed with reading chair, bookcases, and overflowing, disorganized desk. Dave might sign a recently released book, talk about how he's fed up with the poetry published in literary magazines today, and muse about his favorite Midwestern poets, Edgar Lee Masters and Carl Sandburg.

In the last letter I received from Dave, in April 2006, nine years before he died, he reveals, "Yes, I am very much writing poems and smoking much, much less. Don't want my heart doctor getting himself all bent out of shape. If I live to be 100—or even 90—I will tell everyone I owe it to smoking my pipe as much as possible and in writing poems—two things they will know nothing about."

FIVE: The Reviewer

I need no private detective to find E. Lewis; the internet proves sleuth enough. After culling several misses when googling "E. Lewis," I try "E. Lewis, Elburn, il" and find an Emily E. Lewis and a Michael Lewis with a phone number and Elburn zip code, along with information they also lived in Lanark, Illinois, where Dave last lived.

The Gates Street address sounds as familiar as an Elvis classic. I Google Map it, afraid and excited in equal measure at where the red teardrop will point.

And there it is, northwest of Elburn's downtown. With two fingers I scroll closer, closer, closer, until I'm on top of the house where Dave lived before moving west where houses and taxes were cheaper, and where he died in 2015. Soon after he moved, I asked in a letter what was shaking in Lanark. "Not much, no names or pictures in the papers, no midnight calls for help, no drive-by shootings of East Coast poets living in New Jersey. Dull times, these."

But his family, or part of it, might still live in the Elburn house. Had Dave's daughter, Emily, married a Lewis? My hunt for the name ended in a Schwarz Funeral Home obituary for Dave, July 10, 2015:

> *Dave Etter is survived by his wife, Peggy to who [sic] he was married to since 1959. Also, daughter Emily Etter (Michael) Lewis....*

E. Lewis=Emily Etter Lewis. Coincidence? Possibly. I wanted it to be. But all indications suggested my selling the books Dave signed had provoked a daughter's wrath, spurred her to attack me as a poet and person because, to her, I had betrayed Dave's friendship. It didn't matter that Dave and I conversed for hours about music and poetry; didn't matter we shared readings and signings; didn't matter I wrote several reviews of his books; didn't matter we shared handwritten (mine) and typewritten (his) letters; didn't matter that I valued Dave as a friend, mentor, and muse.

What mattered was Emily believed I'd heartlessly and greedily sold the books for financial gain.

SIX: The Meeting

It never happened. And never will, unless Emily and I run into each other at the Jewel two blocks from where she lives.

My first instinct upon discovering E. Lewis's identity was to call her, explain why I sold Dave's books. Tell her I was sorry.

I couldn't. And yet, I couldn't just drop it. E. Lewis's vitriol nagged; her accusations festered. Was her anger warranted and justified, or was it misplaced and overwrought? Should I feel guilty and ashamed, or attacked and abused?

SEVEN: The Price

Looking on the internet for the title of a poem Dave dedicated to me, I came across an Uncharted Books ad.

> ***ETTER, Dave [SIGNED]***
> ***12 Inscribed First Edition Poetry Books by Dave Etter***
>
> *This is a lot of 12 first edition poetry chapbooks and books by beloved Midwestern poet Etter, including uncommon first editions of* Alliance, Illinois *and* I Want to Talk About You. *All are association copies inscribed to Etter's friend,*

fellow Illinois poet Rick Holinger. All of these books are in very good condition with minor shelf wear.

What follows is a listing and description of each book, then the *coup de grace*:

Price: $350.00

Maybe I should buy them back. But for whom? Me? Emily? Dave?

Annoyed, confused, and solemn, I left the posting.

EIGHT: The Three Graces

I am struck by E. Lewis's use of "grace" in her Amazon review's first sentence, "*I dislike that this hack passes himself as a poet and a [sic] attempts to work himself into the good graces of real poets.*" I'm okay with her calling me a hack; she is entitled to her opinion, regardless of whether judging the quality of the poetry—or the personality of the poet.

It's her use of "the good graces" catches my attention most.

> *The Three Graces*
> *...goddesses of grace and beauty. They presided over the dance, the banquet, and all social pleasures. Their names are Aglaia, brilliancy; Euphrosyne, mirth; and Thalia, the blooming. They are usually described as in the service of other divinities, and are patrons of music, eloquence, poetry, and all arts that delight and elevate.*

E. Lewis would have her readers believe I purposefully attached myself to Dave to feed off his reputation; squirmed to get inside Dave's skin to leech there; spent time visiting, reading, and writing about Dave and his work not to "delight and elevate," but instead to deceive, to burrow into his graces, his home, his family.

No, E. Lewis, just no. I valued and cherished Dave's "brilliancy, mirth, and blooming." I loved his baritone laughter flowing out with a tsunami of joy; I loved listening to him read from *Alliance, Illinois,* filling me as with the rapture of a presence of a divine. No. I was not there to horn in or to beguile.

I was there because I loved the man—and his poetry.

NINE: The House Today

I drive to Elburn's locally renown Ream's Meat Market. It is fall, described by Dave in a 2003 letter, "so quiet in this part of town you can hear the leaves whisper to each other and tell dirty jokes and repeat old stories. There are no people around. Do they know something I don't know? Most of the people here are on the government's Witness Protection Program, and I know they think I am also."

Leaving town, I impulsively turn off Main Street and inch down a tree-lined street until I see what used to be Dave's house. It's newly painted white. It looks happy. I consider walking up to the house and ringing the doorbell. Finding E. Lewis at home, she asks if I want iced tea, coffee or, why not, a beer? We sit on the porch where her father and I once sat. We reminisce, tell stories about her father that make us laugh and cry. An hour later, I say I need to go. We hug and say, Let's do this again. I wave goodbye. E. Lewis raises her empty beer glass in farewell.

The vision vanishes. I make a U-turn and head back to Main Street. Looking straight ahead, I know that even if I were to check, the house would not be there, would never be there again.

It's My Novel! It's My Thesis! It's My Novel AND My Thesis!

I pour over the 56-page book on *Formal Requirements for the Partial Completion of the Doctoral...* blah, blah, blah. To ensure compliance and accuracy, I call the office.

"Graduate College," a woman answers.

"Hi. I'm a Ph.D. candidate in English with a creative writing emphasis and am writing a novel for my dissertation."

"You are writing a thesis," she corrects me.

"Right. On my acknowledgements page, I mention two books referenced in the novel. Do I need to do anything else?"

"You need to cite them as you would when writing a thesis."

"This is a novel."

"It is a thesis."

"Do I need a Works Cited page?"

"All outside sources must be cited."

"I need parenthetical documentation in my novel?"

"In your thesis."

"Won't that break the willing suspension of disbelief?"

"You are writing a thesis."

I call my dissertation advisor.

"You shouldn't have said anything," he says. "Your conscientiousness has gotten you in trouble. Cite the sources."

I add a Works Cited page and go to her office. Outside, I hear the person I talked to on the phone tell someone his thesis needs better quality bond and whiter paper.

Inside, a middle-aged woman, impeccably dressed, sits behind a large desk. "You may sit down." I hand her my thesis and a copy. "You typed the title page information upside down on the manilla envelope."

"I didn't know there was an up and down."

She holds the manilla envelope's flap. "The microfilm people want to know what's up and what's down, so pages don't fall out. You put the flap through the typewriter first."

"Will the hook go through?"

"It goes through mine." She grimaces. "Why are the chapter headings on the left margin?"

Because it's a novel; they go where I want them to go. "I don't know."

"Chapter headings should be centered."

"That wasn't specified in your precious format book," I want to say.

"How many chapters are there?"

"Twenty-eight."

"Why so many?"

"Because it's a novel."

"It is a thesis."

At home, I correct the thesis on my TRS-80 (a.k.a. "Trash-80") computer but can't center the chapter headings. Frustrated and furious, I call the format person.

"There's no space left on my disks for me to block pages in order to print them. Could I delete the chapter headings, or, possibly, leave them the way they are?"

Silence. Then, "I would have typed the pages that had headings on a separate disk."

"I wish I had talked to you when I was typing this up." I try to keep the hostility out of my voice, try to sound humble, thankful.

"There's only one thing we can do. Add a disclaimer stating your thesis does not conform to the correct format."

Home free. When I return a few days later with the corrected thesis, she begins shuffling pages. Neither of us speaks. I feel like a cancer patient awaiting the test results from his oncologist.

She focuses on one page of the thesis. "What style sheet did you use?"

"The one the Graduate College handed out."

"No, you didn't."

Yes, I did. I say nothing.

"Why isn't the chapter title in capital letters?"

BECAUSE IT'S A NOVEL, I think, but smile instead.

"Why no regular chapter titles? 'Chapter 1.' What does that tell anyone about the chapter?"

Dickens used those exact chapter titles for *Great Expectations*. But that was a novel.

"Someone else came in here with the same kind of thesis. His chapter titles were not the word 'Chapter,' but descriptions of what were to be found in the chapters."

"Names for the chapters."

"Then you know what the chapter is about. Look at your table of contents." She holds up the page. "'Chapter 1. Chapter 2.' You don't know what the chapter is about."

"Hmmm. I see what you mean."

She flips through the rest of the thesis and then closes it. She announces that I will not have to capitalize each letter in the word ‘chapter’ or add descriptions. I can go.

“Thank you,” I say. “I learned something today.”

“That’s why we’re here.” She cocks her head with the satisfaction of having taught well. “We’re a learning institution.”

TRAVELS HERE AND THERE

The Art of Passivity

"Are you gonna be here for the next few minutes?"

I look up from grading research papers, the late ones, the worst ones, the ones written hurriedly or were plagiarized, the long, undocumented paragraphs reading like Walter Isaacson, because they could be Walter Isaacson.

A shorter, younger, thinner Lance Armstrong wearing a two-day shadow stands in front of me. Flip-flops, Bermuda shorts—or what passes for them today—green sweatshirt, and burgundy baseball cap with an intricate letter logo looking like a T and an S having excellent sex. He is one of maybe 150 passengers waiting at the gate to board the Southwest Airlines flight from Buffalo to Chicago. Before standing, he had been sitting in the last seat in the row perpendicular to ours, two arm lengths away. The year is the year before TSA agents begin scanning bags, barefeet, and policing for fluids, secluding everyone who passes in a separate room.

"Um, yeah," I say. I mean, where am I going? My wife, Tia, has just left for the restroom, and we'll be boarding in ten minutes. She left me guarding her purse and our seats, so I'm stuck here.

"Would you mind keeping an eye on my stuff?" He holds up a lime-green translucent tube. "I just want to go fill my water bottle."

Without thinking (it's a habit), I bark, "Sure," a Golden Retriever trying to please, happy to fulfill expectations, wanting to be liked.

Then he is gone, and I'm staring at what he left for me to guard, his stuff so close I could kick the pair of shiny white running shoes tied to the gray, bulging backpack leaning against a navy-blue duffle bag named "Niagara University."

It takes ten seconds for me to realize there might be a bomb inside any or all of the items, including the shoes. What I've done is exactly what a terrorist would ask me to do if he or she wanted to plant an explosive in the Buffalo airport. How many times have squawky admonitions in stations and airports insisted, "Report any suspicious activity to authorities;" "Be vigilant;" and "Wake up and smell the fucking roses."

Most people today have learned not to ask strangers to keep an eye on unattended bags, and most people have learned not to accept that responsibility. Unaccompanied bags are the modus operandi of low-incentive terrorists like the Boston Marathon bombers. My diminutive Lance Armstrong looked and behaved like he kept up with today's terrorist zeitgeist, which suggested he was no naïve, long-distant runner who needed to fill his water bottle, but a fanatic bent on drawing an unsuspecting American into his demonic plan.

My imagination's x-ray vision inspects the backpack and duffle bag and sees hundreds of nails ready to spray across the room, on a cell phone's launch. Like steel sparks exploding outward from a bursting firework, they spear the flesh and bone of my fellow passengers waiting to board. I turn to look for Lance, so I can retrieve him, but he's vanished, confirming he's ISIL or Taliban or kook. He successfully picked out the biggest dupe, recognized by his thinning, snowy, Robert Frost hair, button-down shirt, khaki pants, and white canvas tie sneakers. "This moron will accede to anything," Lance surely sized me up. "He'd conform to the will of a goat."

The question becomes not "Are there bombs about to explode?", but "What do I do now?" I go over my options quickly, as who knows when he'll detonate his artful packages?

Option 1: Sit there and wait for the bombs to go off. I like this option. My death will be quick and painless. Unless, I concede, 3,000 nails find my calves and thighs to nest in, leaving me a paraplegic.

Option 2: The right thing, the correct thing, the legalistic thing: March over to the woman behind the desk who prepares to board us. "You might want to check those bags for bombs," I'd tell her. What then? Flight delay or cancellation. Robots and/or dogs brought to check the suspicious articles. Stuck for four hours in a neon-lit, two-way mirrored room where TSA agents interrogate me about why I agreed to watch a stranger's bags, leading to a possible criminal record.

Option 3: Take Tia's purse and my backpack and seek refuge behind the nearest wall, hoping it's a supporting wall that won't disintegrate upon a percussive impact, and listen for the explosion from a position of relative safety. I tell myself this is a coward's way out, a selfish act of self-survival, a throwing over of my fellow passengers. Additionally, this scenario has me shirking my duty, going back on a promise that, even given to a terrorist, is still a promise that I'd keep my eye on his stuff. And what if I missed Tia coming back from the women's restroom, only to have her sit by the danger, worrying where I'd gone, the first to receive the bomb's deathly deliverance? I'd feel really bad.

I run the options through my mind again and again. Which to choose? I turn around again, hoping to see Lance striding back, water bottle filled, a smile on his face thanking me silently for my vigil. But he's nowhere in sight, confirming his diabolical plan. I have to decide. Do I do what's easiest, what's right, or what's selfish?

If you've stayed with this me up to now, surely you guessed that I do nothing. Yes, I continue to sit there, ready to be deafened, then filled with lead or obliterated into shreds smaller and less meaty than shaved beef.

Nonetheless, one benefit results. Three minutes earlier, grading research papers had been drudgery worse than pouring hot tar, but now, simply being alive and not in pain, what once felt like a chore has turned boon; I don't exactly indulge in the pleasure of grading papers, but it's better than dying ignominiously.

Of course, a few minutes later Lance returns, his water bottle brimming. Without saying "Thanks," he sits back down, and I continue grading. When Tia comes back and Lance gets up to board, I'm too ashamed to tell her what just occurred. Not until the next morning, when we're in the kitchen getting ready to leave for our respective teaching jobs, do I reveal the story.

"That was stupid," she affirms, then adds speculatively, "maybe he was an undercover TSA agent doing research on how gullible people are. Or maybe he really was a terrorist testing out ploys to get people to watch their stuff." Then she asked, "Did he get on board the flight?"

He did, I answer. I know for sure he did, because during the flight I had to stand in the aisle while a woman by the window went to the bathroom. Looking at the other passengers, I discovered Lance a few rows back, his burgundy hat still riding his head, the TS or ST logo still a mystery.

That day, in my high school English classes, I tell them the story. They like it because it's self-deprecating, and who doesn't like hearing their teacher behaved like an irresponsible coward? But I also tell it because I want to stress the theme of carpe diem. A popular senior at our school was killed the Friday before in a freak parking lot accident, the very day we'd left for Buffalo for our daughter's graduate school graduation. He'd been riding on the running board of a large, slow-moving SUV when the driver turned sharply. The kid fell off, and given a hundred ways he could have fallen and walked away with scrapes, he landed on his head, was airlifted to a nearby trauma center, and died that Monday morning.

Earlier in the year we'd read the Romantics, Thoreau and Emerson, along with Jon Krakauer's *Into the Wild*. We watched Robin Williams wow his classes in *Dead Poets Society* reciting "To His Coy Mistress," impressing students with life's brevity. Recently we'd covered the Modernists, William Carlos Williams urging readers in his American vernacular to notice red wheelbarrows glazed with rainwater beside white chickens, to listen for the gong of fire engines, and to taste the delicious plum while eating it. Given the abrupt ending to this young man's life, I wanted to impress on these 16 and 17-year-olds that Horace's ode had it right: don't bank on next winter but rather prune your trees today.

In my honors English class, when I get to the part about Lance's mysterious logo on his baseball cap, kids started searching online possibilities and holding up their finds.

"Like this?"

"No."

"Like this?"

"No."

"Is it like this?"

A boy sitting in the front row holds up his screen. I glance down, and there's Lance's burgundy hat and logo.

Thrilled, I yell, "What is it?"

"Florida State."

I study the F, so shrouded by the baroque S that its lower staff gets lost, leaving the impression of a T. Mystery solved.

"If he's from Florida State," another student queries, "why's he flying from Buffalo to Chicago?"

Better to leave an essay with at least one question unanswered, leaving the reader wanting more, asking more.

Receptions: Poetry, the White House, and the Hostage Trees

Thursday, January 3, 1980

Received two months earlier:

Mrs. Carter
requests the pleasure of your company
at a reception to be held at
The White House
on Thursday afternoon, January 3, 1980
at four o'clock

Above Mrs. Carter's name, gold stars circle a gold eagle on a white card heavy enough to patch a roof. In the envelope's upper left corner, in gold, the return address only THE WHITE HOUSE, as if to tell postal carriers, "You know where to find us."

We arrive fifteen minutes early, 3:45, at the Southwest entrance and join a line already formed along the black fence. Standing behind a man wearing blue corduroy cutoffs and hiking boots, we wonder if we're overdressed in semi-formal attire. At four o'clock, the line, two or three people thick, shuffles forward. Three guards are checking identification while a fourth talks to the occasional limousine pulling up.

Reaching the gatehouse, we show our driver's licenses; those without must give their social security number, which begins a five-minute wait while the guard calls a federal government branch (FBI? CIA?) for identity confirmation. Can't be too careful with poets and their ilk.

I recognize Doug, a friend I haven't seen since grade school, and we meet his wife, Lenore, a patron of the arts. Her work for the Poetry Foundation and, surely, a contribution, has landed them here. Inside the grounds, walking toward the entrance, I notice the lawn looks vaster than on TV, and except for a small guardhouse, security seems lax.

"One could run amok here," Doug says. It's maybe thirty degrees, but there's no snow, and the grass is greener than the fir trees.

We're directed to small double doors east of the two grand spiral staircases reserved, we suppose, for something more ceremonious than the arrival of poets and fans of poetry. Inside, we're handed a program and asked to choose one of the seven rooms listed; under each are listed three poets scheduled to read there. The only room already filled promises James Dickey, the Robert Frost of our day. (In 1974, when I was a graduate student at Washington University, poet—and then professor—Howard Nemerov arranged a reading by Dickey in the school's chapel. Rumor had it he flew first class to St. Louis and was paid $10,000 for a forty-five-minute reading, my annual salary at the private school where I taught five years later.)

We choose the Blue Room, featuring John Ciardi, Gwendolyn Brooks, and Richard Eberhart. Brooks hails from my hometown,

Chicago; Ciardi, from what I've read of his poetry and prose, comes across as a Renaissance man; and the little Eberhart I'd read I liked. Waiting on metal folding chairs, we overhear the people coming in after us complaining they stood in line for forty-five minutes. We hear some poets scheduled to read showed up never having RSVPed, the CIA trying to confirm their identity. Perhaps the Marines stationed at the front gate should have prepared for tonight by studying back-cover author photographs of the poets' skinny volumes.

Finally, Ciardi stands, first to take the Blue Room's lectern. "If I have any energy left after standing in line," he quips, "I'll read three poems." Eberhart follows with "Fury of Aerial Bombardment," and Brooks includes her classic, "We Real Cool."

Throughout the readings, loud clapping from the adjoining Red and Green Rooms eclipse many of our poets' lines, so we, in turn—in retaliation?—clap insatiably at the end of each work. After half an hour of vicious ovations, our poets finished reading, a Marine guard in dress blues invites us to follow him to The East Room, already crowded from Dickey's reading where, naturally, he's been given the largest room.

Beneath three huge chandeliers, we are part of the standing-room-only audience in the back of the room, fit between wide wooden boxes supporting TV cameras, bright lights, and photographers with arm-length lenses. Up front, Mrs. Carter and daughter Amy appear on a foot-high platform, perhaps where once Baryshnikov danced. The First Lady invites the poets who performed to please line up behind her on stage. Each, when introduced, steps forward, but many are absent, still dispensing their wares. Only the elders, the veteran poets who've been ceremoniously honored before, look at ease.

In a short address, Mrs. Carter tells us poetry can enrich lives, make sad people happy, and give meaning to life. She tries to sound erudite and pithy, but she comes across like a five-year-old explaining blank verse to Shakespeare. She reminisces about the times after dinner Jimmy would read poems to his family and then discuss them. She ends by saying there will be a receiving line in the hall outside the room, on the way to the reception, if we would like to participate, and then leaves with Joan Mondale, the vice president's wife, followed by the featured poets.

The hallway leads to the State Dining Room where, we are told, refreshments wait. All 500 of us fall in line to meet the First and Second Ladies when we overhear someone say, "The President's here!" Rumor has it he's been working in the Oval Office on the Iranian hostage crisis and has decided to take a break.

I ask Tia what she's going to say in the five seconds she has with the most powerful man on earth. Running through about twenty things myself, they all sound trite, just what I, as part of a contingency of poets, should be able to avoid.

A Marine guard stands on our side of President and Mrs. Carter. "Should we give our names?" I ask.

"You may if you wish," he replies. "But this is an informal receiving line."

No, in other words. What tact—nothing stated in the negative.

Tia approaches, shakes hands with the president. "I'm a foreign language teacher," she says, "and I would like to thank you for what you've done in the past year for foreign languages."

He answers, but his southern accent and the din of voices obscures his answer.

Instead of a polite, polished, “Excuse me, sir?” or “Pardon me?”, Tia bursts out, "What?!"

This flusters him. Carter grins more broadly than his polite meet’n-greet-smile ordinarily allows and says again, "Ah hawts ah in it." (Translation: “Our hearts are in it.”)

Comrades in confusion, they are still shaking hands after the exchange, Carter smiling.

My turn. I step forward. The president is a short man, maybe five and a half feet, and slight. All the reports are true: he does have a terrific smile and incredibly kind eyes. Or maybe that’s just what I wanted to see in my President.

"Thank you," I begin, "for all you've done for all the arts."

I have no recollection of his reply, and I have nothing left for Mrs. Carter or Mrs. Walter Mondale, so I go with "So nice to be here," or something equally inane. Tia, who also teaches art, tells Mrs. Mondale, "Nice to have a ceramicist here." She laughs as she replies, "You betcha!"

Later, over appetizers, Doug tells us he was ready to tell the president, "It was nice of you to come," but the president said it first, which wrecked everything. Bill and his wife, Dorothy, missed him the first time through, so they went through again. "We wanted," they said to Mrs. Carter the second time through, "to meet your husband."

The reception in the State Dining Room, which included Almaden wine, crackers, and cheese squiggles, must have been planned to make poets and poetry audiences feel at home, the smoked salmon, caviar, and champagne kept on ice for People Who Counted. We mingle, most of The Great Ones standing in place, putting up with beginners like me. I want to shake the hands that have held the pens that have made money from poetry. Most male poets, even if their faces are unrecognizable, wear the uniform—sports jacket, striped shirt, and comfortable pants.

I approach the few poets I know.

The first, John Morris, I know from taking his Milton class at Washington University. In his sixties or early seventies, he resembles an Oxford don. A habitual smoker in both the classroom and office, between puffs in class one day he asked me to talk about the diction in a particular stanza of *Paradise Lost*. Not having been an English major in college, and having no idea what "diction" meant, I stammered until rescued by one of my peers, leading to one of my many Bs in graduate school, when As are expected. His recent poetry book, a switch from Milton scholasticism, won wide critical praise. Tonight, he let me in on why his poetic colleagues (and my former teachers) Howard Nemerov and Donald Finkel hadn't come. "They said, 'It costs a lot to come to Washington.'"

Poet Robert ("rp") Dana, who five years ago married Peg Sellen, a woman with whom I shared graduate classes, is asking his fellow poets to sign his program; he shows me the seventeen signatures he's procured so far.

Donald Hall, whom I've never met but have long savored "Kicking the Leaves," says he lives in New Hampshire now, no longer teaches, and loves it. He adds that ironically, although he's only half an hour's drive from Maxine Kumin, he's met her here for the first time tonight, in Washington, D.C.

Robert Hayden, nearly blind, wears thick lenses in black fames. His wife leads him from group to group. He wears not the male poet's uniform, but a smart black suit and conservative tie. Bill, who knows him from teaching at the

University of Michigan, tells me the poet's not well, perhaps why his wife supports him as he walks. When Bill stops Hayden and introduces me on his way out, the poet says kindly, "I'm sure I'll read your work someday." I marvel that in the minute he's known me he has picked up on my intelligence, genius, and passion; he's picked me out as a rising newcomer, one destined to be one of the Greats.

A few minutes later, I hear Hayden talking to the gathering next to ours, his warm, mellifluous voice telling a fledgling poet, "I'm sure I'll read your work someday."

We tell Gwendolyn Brooks we're from Chicago, as if that will endear us to her, and then introduce her to a couple we've run into from Winnetka as if, just having met her, we're old pals.

I remind Ted Weiss that I met him at a reception given for him at Washington University after a reading he gave. Trying to impress him with my fandom, I ask how his next novel is going. He responds that he's never written a first one.

We spot Very Famous Poets from a distance too intimidating to approach: James Dickey with a gorgeous young woman beside him; Richard Eberhart, dressed to the nines—or tens—like Wallace Stevens, V.P. of Hartford Accident and Indemnity Company; and John Ashberry, looking younger than his mythological status, wearing gold-rimmed glasses.

I'm at ease only when talking to the servers. I ask a man dressed in black behind the long food and wine table how often they have parties like this.

"Oh, four or five times a week, once or twice a day."

Suddenly this special occasion seems less special.

On the outskirts of the crowd, a Marine guard sips a glass of wine. Tia and I tell him we're glad he's loosening up, but it's hard to think of questions to ask without sounding like a spy digging for secrets. We ask anyway. Remembering how the President seemed to materialize in the receiving line, we pry, "How does the president arrive?"

"By elevator." The guard smiles perfectly. "We make room for him. Most groups are very nice. Some push back. This crowd is especially nice, one of the best we've had in a long time."

We ask what's behind the lighted windows we can see outside.

"The President's office. The Oval Office."

From where, the very next night, Carter will deliver his speech in response to the Russian invasion of Afghanistan and the suspension of trade with the U.S.S.R., the speech he was probably working on when he took a break to meet a cadre of poets. Next afternoon, on the way to the airport to fly home to Chicago, we'll see a CBS TV film truck outside the gate surrounded by sniffing dogs.

After the reception, we're invited to wander through rooms named not for kings and queens as in Europe, but for colors, direction, and purpose. They seem too small to carry their historic and aesthetic burdens. Somebody nearby says it's this very fact that defines democracy, something magnificent, but not ostentatious. Even though we've heard The White House is our home, America's home, I don't feel at home. The formal and expensive antiques—paintings, vases, and furniture—dispels any homey feeling—but I also don't feel out of place. Even though my grandparents had died by the time I was three, I imagine this feeling, this experience, might be like going to one's grandparents' house for Thanksgiving when a child, the surroundings marvelous because simultaneously familiar and foreign. The fact that we are one of many groups of poets (published or not) and poetry readers, instills a festive and cohesive feeling. We are children playing with words, lines, and sounds finally recognized, perhaps even praised, by the elders.

The crowd thins. We exit downstairs, through the Diplomatic Room (an irony perhaps not lost on the nation's writers who often pride themselves on their lack of diplomacy). On our walk to the gate, we look back at The White House, brilliantly lit against the backdrop of night. Turning again to leave, we see the Washington Monument needling the dark. Closer to us, cloaked by night, fifty small fir trees glow with blue and white lights, one planted for each American hostage in Iran, an idea that might sound trite in print, but seen on a night like this, in a time such as this, the pines work their magic on us.

We wander silently out past the blue trees, darkened gardens, silhouetted fence, and security shack. If looking back, like Orpheus and Eurydice, I fear finding everything has vanished.

Angel of the Black Hills

My wife, Tia, speaks French with a thirty-something Wild Bill Hickok doppelganger. He sports the iconic mustache and goatee. Long, straight hair capes his shoulders. On his head, a white straw cowboy hat with red band touts the tour company's name. A Western snap-button shirt accompanies white cotton pants bunched in waves at the waist where a black belt notched beyond factory-bored holes suggests he recently dropped fifty pounds. Laced brown hiking boots finish his neo-cowboy look.

"This is Raphael," Tia says.

He opens the Jeep's rear door and takes out a metal step for Tia and me, both in our sixties, to climb in, Tia in a small back seat, me, with longer legs, in front. Inside, it's stifling. Outside, the morning has reached maybe sixty degrees with overcast, drizzly skies. We head south out of Rapid City on a four-lane.

A week ago, Tia and I turned in our high school students' final grades. Neither of us had taken family trips as kids to the Badlands and Mt. Rushmore. After three days of driving and sightseeing, we wanted someone to guide us through South Dakota's Black Hills.

National chain stores and mini-malls vanish as four lanes shrink to two, and we wind up and down through lush green woods.

"How'd you get to South Dakota?" Tia asks.

"My dad was a jazz musician living in New York City," Raphael says. "I grew up with my mom in France. When visiting Dad, I went along when he toured with his band. When nineteen, I took a bus to the Grand Canyon and ran out of money, but got to Porcupine, South Dakota, where I lived on the Pine Ridge Reservation for a couple of years as an intern, part of my graduate studies in International Affairs. I learned the Lakota Sioux language and culture.

"Pine Ridge Rez," Raphael continues, "has the highest suicide rate and the worst poverty in the country. But the Lakota taught me to form a positive outlook out of dire circumstances."

When Tia says she teaches art, Raphael mentions Hill City, where he knows the owner of Dahl Gallery.

"I was surprised at all the culture—art, music, dance—more than just rodeos," he laughs. "In winter, people get lots of time to get creative."

Dark green pine and deciduous woods thicken on both sides of the road.

"The Black Hills are spiritual to the Lakota," Raphael says. "When Custer found gold here, he made it sound much more than it was to draw settlers."

Low, misty clouds blanket the hills, their summits lost. We pass Mt. Rushmore's turn-off and the traffic disappears.

"We are going to Needles Highway," he says. "Peter Norbeck, a United States senator, in the 1930s designed a road people thought couldn't be built. His road was not meant to go anywhere. He wanted to emphasize nature."

Raphael paused. "There is white time and there is Native American time. In a class I took, the Lakota teacher didn't start right in lecturing. We first did smudging, burning sage to get rid of the negative energies. Then we smelled some sweetgrass to draw in the positive energies. Next, the teacher asked, 'How ya doin'?' to which everyone responded not by just saying 'Fine,' but actually telling stories. It's not a waste of time. Your grade wasn't based on papers, like most schools. Students worked in social services. We used our knowledge in real life.

"The Lakota have lots of virtues. They joke about something someone said, then leave a space before they laugh. They laugh with the person, even if the joke is on him. They want to see if he can take the joke. When I first started hanging out with the Lakota, the older men would make a joke about me, and I wouldn't know how to take it. Then they said, 'If we didn't like you, we would ignore you.'

"All this is part of your education. Everything is story. Stories make you think. When the story gets to the end, you wait for the punch line, but it doesn't come."

Is he putting us on? Telling us Lakota stories have no ending, no conclusion, that their meanings have to be intuited? Is he setting us up for a story without a point, just to have us try to make one up? Or is he helping us, protecting our egos, letting us know that if we don't get a Lakota story, we shouldn't feel bad?

"I will tell you a story. Today's Lakota believe we live in the fourth or fifth world. A long time ago, in a world before ours, everyone was equal, animals and humans. The four-legged land animals thought they were stronger, faster, and better than the puny two-legged animals.

"'We should impose our world on them,' the four-legged animals thought. 'We're taking over, but we should give the two-legged animals a fair shot to prove they are better.'

"So the humans discussed what to do. The elders, chiefs, and everyone else held a meeting. They reached a consensus when they realized, 'We're screwed.'

"One guy on the outskirts of the group didn't say much. Finally, he said, 'Why not challenge the four-legged animals to a race?' 'Okay,' said the wise people, not coming up with anything better.

"So they sent a messenger to the animal people. The race would be to run around the Black Hills. The humans said, 'If you win, you rule; if we win, we all stay equal.'

"The race begins. The mountain lion shoots out front, but the odds are on the wolf to win, because it has endurance. The humans start out running hard but drop off and eventually end up behind.

"Meanwhile, the animals start competing with each other. The antelope is the second fastest animal on earth after the cheetah, but he has no endurance. The coyote takes shortcuts. Halfway there, the horses are out front because they run on the flat land around the Black Hills. By now, the mountain lion has piddled out.

"They come to the final turn toward home. The humans are not in any rearview mirror. They were running as fast as they could, but everyone was competing with themselves, no one working together.

"Meanwhile, the birds were watching from above. "'Hey, look at that!' said a nation of magpies. ‘I don’t know if we should let this happen. After all, we’re two-legs, too.’

“So the magpies joined the race.”

The car goes silent, only the low whine of the engine filling the stillness. Outside, low clouds obscure rock cliffs and narrow gorges.

I don’t know what to say. I don’t want to suggest a moral just to have Raphael mock my interpretation. “I see why you think Lakota stories have morals,” I try.

“The story can be told with a variance, with eagles, not magpies.”

Is he calling Tia and me magpies? Confused and frustrated, I say nothing.

“The figure four carries significance,” he adds cryptically. “The story is symbolic. Animals with feathers count for much, evidence of the importance of birds.”

At a wooden sign announcing “Norbeck Wildlife Preserve,” we turn onto a steep, twisting, narrow Needles Highway. The Jeep grudgingly grinds upward through towering firs, long needle pines, and green-leafed canopy.

“We’ll stop for lunch at Subway,” Raphael says. “And have a picnic at Sylvan Lake.”

We reach the town of Custer and drive down its broad main street. Population, 1,860. It looks like any small Midwestern town: two-story, flat-front, awning or porch-filled brick facades braying the names of bars, restaurants, variety stores, banks, antique shops, and other businesses.

We pass a Subway, triggering my asking, “Were we going to stop for lunch?”

Raphael makes a U-turn. “These streets are wide because that’s what it took to turn around a wagon train.”

Back in the wooded hills, Raphael points out distant massive, spear-like rock formations we'll eventually climb to as we follow a small stream. We are in the clouds, above 6,000 feet. Valleys vanish.

"A Lakota creation story should take a year to tell," Raphael says. "'Inyan' means rock, stone. Thunder Bean. Thunder Cloud. Cathedral Spires. Eye of the Needle."

I'm silenced by his mishmash of words. Tall rock columns spear a hundred feet or more into a cloud, then disappear. The rocky phallic erectile symbolism surely contributes to the tribe's continuation.

"For the Lakota to sell these mystical spires is as likely as Catholics selling the Vatican. 'Where the thunders meet the rocks.'"

We park and Raphael leads us across the road. "Look up."

Above us, a dark oval monolith wider than a redwood tree marks the spiritual heart of the Lakota Sioux. The Eye of the Needle—a slit in the upper part of the column where a white cloud contrasts the shiny, mist-blackened rock. Tia and I regard it as the sacred center Raphael purports it to be, and then we slide farther down the mountain.

Sylvan Lake, seen through a veil of pine trees and soft rain, looks like a place where Hobbits might stroll and dragons drink. At a picnic table we eat our sandwiches.

"There are four or five weddings a week here," Raphael says. "A lot of trailheads start here, one to Harney Peak. The Lakota want to change its name to Black Elk Peak, because this is where Black Elk had his vision."

The iconic text *Black Elk Speaks* describes the unity of all earth's people. "...then he saw the sacred hoop of earth mended," Raphael summarizes. "The tree of life had left a few roots, and the children gathered. Black Elk was amazed because there were more than just red children. He saw that all the people of the earth were united."

We turn into the entrance to Crazy Horse Memorial. Inside the spacious, pine-paneled Crazy Horse Center, the Indian Museum of North America, a life-size teepee, buffalo, and horse dominate the room beneath a pine cathedral ceiling. I mosey to a glass display case and find a tomahawk pipe, a palpable symbol of humankind's dual nature of war and peace.

From the outdoor wood-slat deck, the Viewing Veranda, on a clear day we could see the mountain-carved sculpture of Crazy Horse's face on a hill maybe five miles away. Today a cloud veils the statue, so we rely on a snow-white 1-to-34-foot scale model of his head and planned torso astride a galloping horse, the Indian's left arm stretched out, its index finger pointing forward.

"Daniel is starting," Raphael urges. "Too bad it's drizzling. He usually dances out here."

Inside a room the size of a basketball court, backless benches are filled with mostly EuroAmerican tourists of all ages. Facing them, a tall man with wide shoulders and large chest addresses the crowd. Maybe in his early sixties, he's dressed in fringed yellow shirt and pants. Along one pant leg, the silhouette of a huge spider crawls before two cryptic images, one resembling a bat. Daniel's wrap-around sunglasses hide his eyes beneath a yellow headband.

"Thunder Mountain is the center or beginning of earth," Daniel relates about where Crazy Horse is memorialized in stone. "The first few bits of cosmic dust formed here. The particles of dust came together, and earth was formed. The Black Hills is a sacred place. You come here to heal yourself.

"I have spent years teaching. And do you

know the question most people ask? 'What kind of food do Indians eat?' I tell them, 'Pizza and Taco Bell.'"

Laughter.

"The second most-asked question is, 'Do you still live in teepees?' And I say, 'No, there's no place for a satellite TV or hot tub.'"

More laughter.

"The third question they ask most is, 'Are you a real Indian?' And I say, 'What do they look like?'"

Raucous laughter.

"I have yet to meet people who all look alike."

Muted, thoughtful laughter.

Daniel shifts his attention to his attire. "Yellow is the color of the grass dancer. The actions of the dance move and push down grasses. Indians moved a lot and danced down the grasses before putting up the teepees. The bending in the dance symbolizes servitude. We serve our people."

Daniel turns and pushes a button on a large boombox. Out tumble steady, pounding drumbeats. Suddenly, as if punched, Daniel slumps over and begins to stomp on the pine floor with his moccasins as if putting out a fire. He traipses back and forth, then up and down the rows of benches, behind the boombox, until the drumbeats and his movements stop. We clap, impressed the large elderly man can survive such a workout.

"Nature is our inspiration for dances. The next dance is called the Prairie Chicken Dance. It says, 'Hey check me *out*!' to women, and 'Hey, check *me* out!' to men. The dance is meant to help find a mate."

Over the next few minutes, a cock-sure Daniel strutts around like a proud—and/or horny—prairie chicken.

For the final dance, the Friendship, or Snake Dance, Daniel asks for volunteers. When no one stands up, he starts pointing out victims who smile awkwardly, then acquiesce. Eventually, others come up—dads and daughters, grandparents and grandchildren.

With maybe twenty people lined up behind him, Daniel berates those of us who haven't joined. I feel he has singled me out, so I pretend to take notes and be invested in taking photographs.

"It's easy to take pictures," Daniel says. "It's easy to say, 'We saw a Native today.'"

I lower my head, avoid his gaze. My notes turn into drivel, nonsense sentences to make it look like I'm writing something important. Daniel has shamed me. He has called out my preference for distancing myself from the community, for standing back and observing, for recording events rather than participating. Scared of appearing foolish, of making a mistake, I avoid challenges and new experiences.

Daniel invited me into his world, and I shut his world out. Feeling mortified, now I want to join in, but it's too late.

"We're going to show everyone we can work together," he says. "If we can work together on this little stage, we can work together in the world."

The tape player's drum hammers through the room. He instructs the line to hold hands and, as Daniel leads off, the human snake begins to twist behind him as he weaves in and out of the benches, calling, "We won't break the snake luck!"

They don't; no matter how tightly the serpent winds in on itself, Daniel unwinds it without losing anyone. The snake chortles merrily as Black Elk's vision of acceptance and inclusion coils and uncoils before me.

I am sorry I am not one of them.

Back in the Jeep, I ask Raphael how he and Daniel became friends.

"I was standing by the teepee in the Center watching the Grass and Snake Dances. I waited in line to speak to him. I put a broken cigarette in his hand, and said, 'Thank you.' He looked at me for a long time then said, 'Did you mean that?'

"A broken cigarette is a symbol for thanksgiving. It's not for smoking. When you go to an elder, you bring tobacco or food to honor the person. When he said, 'Did you mean that?' I said, 'Yes.' Then Daniel began to sing. It's the Lakota way of trading. You give more than you receive."

We slide into Hill City. Pickups and SUVs line the main street under a thick, gray sky. After parking on a side street, we walk past a large lawn sign:

FAMILY HAIR CARE
CURL UP & DYE

Inside the art store/gallery we meet Sandra, creator of the artwork displayed on tee-shirts, coasters, greeting cards, and a myriad of other surfaces. I pick out a couple of shirts and a card or two while Tia and Sandra talk artistic process and materials.

Outside, in a small courtyard, three dancers of different ages—youth, middle age, and senior—dressed in gorgeous, colorful attire, dance to a drummer's beat.

Raphael whispers, "We're lucky; they're filming a video to promote some future Native event." The elder dancer's eagle feather headdress reaches down his back to his waist; the middle-aged man carries a spear adorned with eagle feathers; the drummer, a bald man in sunglasses, wears gray slacks and a navy L.L. Bean-style pullover.

Their dances draw me in, embrace me. I want to stay here, want to be part of it, want to feel what they feel.

Driving back to Rapid City, we return through juniper-green forests. “What about the name, Black Hills?” I ask.

“It’s a Native American name. They look black if you’re about thirty to forty miles away.”

Pulling up to the hotel’s door, Tia and I promise to write a commendatory TripAdvisor recommendation, then say “*Au revoir*!” “*A bientot*!”

At home, I research Raphael’s namesake. An archangel in Judaism, Christianity, and Islam, he performs all manners of healing. The forests, the hills, Sonja, Daniel, the the Eye of the Needle, the magical blanched mist—if they did not entirely heal me, they did send me home a different person. Linked to Raphael’s one long dance, I was twisted around and around, trying not to let go, trying my best to hold on.

The Foreign Zoo: Tour(s)ing in Place

We will do anything to stay out of the University of Tours' dormitory. It is dirty, hot, angular, spare, and gray. We are made to feel like interlopers. *La concierge* grumbles when we ask for our mail. The African students who cannot afford to return home for summer vacation sleep until noon, play soccer until five, eat until ten, then sing repetitive lyrics beat out by bongo drums until three in the morning.

Living here is cheaper than a hostel. My wife, Tia, a high school teacher, received a scholarship from the French government to take classes at the university, so her cost is covered. For me, for the month, we're paying the U.S. currency equivalent of eighty dollars, the price of one night in a Paris hotel.

I settle into a routine. By the time we leave the dorm, the bus stopping to pick up campus passengers is full, so we stand for the half hour drive to downtown Tours. The driver fantasizes he's in a Maserati, grinding up and down through the gears and swerving in and out of traffic, throwing us back and forth through air thick with pungent body odor.

When Tia and the other scholarship students leave, I join them, wanting to give them a proper sendoff, their Penelope waving at them from the pier as they disappear into the university's Victorian mansion.

I stroll in my tattered London Fog raincoat, polo shirt, khakis, and running shoes through city streets where shopkeepers hose their sidewalk domain, then sweep with brooms of bundled straw. Sitting outdoors at my favorite café, my French barely good enough to order a *café au lait*, I write in my journal until the coffee drives me downstairs to the Turkish toilet. Grasping the metal handles, I squat over a porcelain hole while trying to direct my urine beneath me, only occasionally missing my pant leg.

Returning to the table, I hear Rod Stewart on the jukebox. In my journal, I continue to record the battle between the African undergraduate students and the American graduate students, waged with slammed doors and cranked-up radios. The weather often rainy, mid-seventies. The Black Forest cake at a nearby *patisserie*. The laundromat in Medieval Tours where a United Nations of ethnic diversity wash and dry clothes. French men don't drink milk because believed proper only for pregnant women. Yellow marigolds, red roses, and myriads of blue and purple flowers flooding the town square and dividing broad avenues. And our return to campus one evening to discover spray-painted on the university's entrance wall, *ICI ZOO ETRANGER* (HERE IS THE FOREIGN ZOO).

Someone begins playing a video game blaring erratic *deet*s. I wander down to *la* *bibliotheque*. My favorite room has windows as tall as four Ping-pong tables stacked end to end overlooking the Loire River where dark, swift birds dart for invisible prey. I command a round table suitable for Arthurian knights situated close to English-written reference books.

I forage through the journal for poetic or fictive subjects. If nothing prompts a new start, rough drafts get revised. Three hours pass in fifteen minutes. Writing does that, takes me out of time, dissolves the physical world. I could be at my desk in northern Illinois or on a walk through a Midwestern floodplain listening to birdsong and creek water splashing over a dam's fish ladder.

At noon, Tia meets me for a picnic in a town square or park. In the afternoons, we do tourist things. We visit not wineries but *caves* (sounds like "cobs"), our favorite in the town of Vouvray. After multiple visits to *les chateaux* of the Loire Valley, we pick Chenonceau our favorite, its curved supporting arches lifting the palace over the river. Inside, tables are inlaid with mosaic bones, and a docent tells about birds who dance to orchestral strings.

After dinner we plan weekend trips. At Cap Ferret, on the Atlantic coast, beneath a gray concrete German pillbox, a beautiful woman leaves her blanket on the beach for the surf where next to me she swims nude. In Paris, two men, looking homeless, argue in enraged voices on opposite sides of the Metro tracks. Above ground, a block of prostitutes in swank evening dresses lean on a Mercedes Benz or BMW.

One day I'm waiting for a bus when an elderly woman asks me directions. I am able to tell her which bus to take. She boards it and disappears. I have finally arrived, am no longer *l'etranger*, am no longer living abroad.

I am merely living.

IT'S COMING BACK TO ME

Controlled Burn

I drive past a field where giant stumps of yellow-helmeted and jacketed workers crop up. Gray smoke rises about them as if secreted from a hundred separate campfires Boy and Girl Scouts keep aflame long enough to qualify for a merit badge. The professional fire fighters/starters stab or spear the earth with flappers to steer flames obediently, and McLeod tools (imagine a rake and hoe making love) to poke in and around, and to remove, earth. Everyone also carries a water backpack with which to extinguish recalcitrant flareups. Like fine, slender lances soldiers have planted to take with them into battle when leaving a keep, brown and black pods surround the workers. For some reason, these plants have survived, either through their own persistence, the fire's path, a burner's choice, or the luck of the wind's draw, so they stretch above the carpet of yellow and orange flames.

I've come to Gray Willows Farm, like most days, to walk. A two-minute drive from my house, this 208-acre farm, sold to the village of Campton Hills in rural northern Illinois, brags 175-year-old maple trees in its thick wood surrounding rolling prairie.

Today, three orange traffic cones seal off the gravel driveway, and the sign,

"CONTROLLED BURN TODAY"

explains why. Mid-November. Figures.

I continue two miles down the road, swing into Corron Farm, another working farm the community purchased. Leaving my sixteen-year-old Prius, I start down one of the broad, mown paths far too well groomed for my taste, but it passes through prairie and skirts deep woods, so I can't complain (too much). I prefer the rustic, gravel-rutted road that Gray Willows Farm offers, its center more crabgrass tufts than golf green. Trails here even have color-coded markers with distances calibrated to a tenth of a percent. With such certitude, where's the pleasure in starting off with a bit of confusion, with looking forward to at least a modicum of surprise, a bit of hardship to overcome?

"Controlled burn," I muse. When teaching forty years of high school English, I should have had an Etsy sticker made with those words blazoned on my blazer when in front of four sections of American lit.

"This is what it's all about," I should have told my charges as they thumb hidden text messages beneath their desks, mumble in their half-sleep, or paste cheat sheets on the soles of their Adidas sneaks to help friends pass a *Grapes of Wrath* quiz. "These authors you're reading, or tell me you've read, to keep their prairies pristine, take the seeds from what's grown before, then scorch what grew before in order to spread, increase, and foster the possible. If they kept it the same, they knew it would rot, would consume itself."

They might leave their texting, their dozing, their cheating, and consider the crazy man behind the desk. Do I have their attention, thanks to the muddle of metaphor? Knowing I'll lose them soon again, I go on.

"Writers scribble or finger a keyboard only when burning controllably—and sometimes, come to think of it, more than sometimes, uncontrollably. They torch the old growth to foster the new with what they picked off the old before laying waste to it. Writing," I pause for effect and raise my voice, "is the act of spilling flame accelerator over dry pine needles in a conifer forest, igniting it, and delighting in the erupting holocaust that wakes imaginary campers from their stupor, and, as they quake before the vision about to be consumed, a safe ending rescues them."

After my walk, I drive home past Gray Willows. Leaden smoke continues to lift from an obsidian field. I imagine this year's first snow falling.

At the end of the first quarter of the twenty-first century, as glaciers slide like waterfalls into the sea, when ice breaks off Antarctica like drydocked ships slipped free, when water levels around the world rise nearly as fast as rivers when dams release their hold, I look forward to the upper Midwest's pearl's snowy solace, however diminutive, however temporary.

Over the winter, I will walk the double-rutted road here and marvel at the rolling landscape stripped of its spring, summer, and fall prairie golds, maroons, cobalts, and emeralds, and I will know that this frozen, barren ensemble is holding its own controlled burn, seething beneath, keen to flare into blossom.

Blowing Toward Winfield

At 25, with a newly printed Master's degree in English, I am out of work when offered a job in Winfield, so I go, even though it is Kansas. On my way by plane in June to the initial interview, I sit beside a woman who tells me I am coming to Kansas at the most spectacular time.

"Why?" I ask, excited.

"Because the wheat is turning from green to gold," she says as a New Englander boasts of his trees.

One does not drive in Kansas. One gets blown from the point of departure to a second point, the point of destination if the wind's right, or one can steer with the tenacity it takes to ride a bull. Hills here are slight rises in the land, jumping off places for the winds. Blowing into Winfield for the first time, I am surprised to see trees, a commodity scarce as conversation in a convent, north, east, and west of the city. A small oasis, a pond of pines among a land of wheat and soybeans.

The wheat is a pale green, and it waves with the wind.

One must drive at least an hour from the nearest interstate to reach Winfield. The second time I blow in, it is August and 103 degrees. The land around Winfield looks like the scene from *The Rifleman* where Lucas rides away from the farm toward town. Because I have thirty-four live plants in my car, the windows are cracked only enough for slight circulation. Not all the plants make it. Some cannot stand the heat and wind.

The first person I see after parking is Pastor Pullman. At three in the afternoon under the bright Kansas sun, even the religious wear sunglasses. I say something about it being hot but not humid.

"It's the weather," he replies.

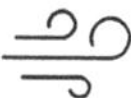

The house I rent is owned by a woman now in a nursing home. Her husband used to march as Uncle Sam in the Labor Day parade. There is a chipping brown swing on the front porch, a rose bedroom with a painting of a cat framed in green above the bed, and a chest made a hundred years ago by Someone in the Family. The living room is Early Musty, the furniture a vomit pink. There are plastic plants everywhere; on the enclosed back porch there are shelves on which stand more plastic flowers, an old Singer sewing machine, and two hand-waving-sized American flags sticking V-shaped in a black wooden paperweight stand. On the walls surrounding a heavy maple desk hang a *Last Supper* with hooded light, a framed facsimile of the *Declaration of Independence*, and the Lord's Prayer hammered in tin.

The toilet overflows the first day. I go next door for a phone. Above several dogs, I hear

"C'mon in! Telephone's through there." The kitchen is misty with flour; pie plates and tin pans range everywhere. The line is busy. She tells me the baking is for the church bazaar tomorrow (she imagines I know which one). She tells me her son is thirty-four and not married, so it is all right that I am not.

I get through to the plumber who says he's my other next-door neighbor and he'll be right over. As I leave, Mrs. Maudsley calls "Come back any time!" and means it.

There is little anonymity in Winfield. Downtown, people welcome me because they don't recognize me and often ask who I am and tell me I must know people who I don't. They tell me they're glad I'm aboard. I feel a sense of community and trust that I never had in New Haven and only occasionally in St. Louis. The people have little to fear; trusting in God, they are in His hands and the world will take shape according to His will. Their celebration is founded in this.

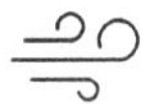

My girlfriend Ann visits from Tulsa, and we pick peaches at Knapp's orchard in Oxford, ten miles west of Winfield. The day is typical: no clouds, over a hundred degrees, windy, but the wind is not strong enough to shake off ripe peaches. The trees themselves are stunning, their fruit hanging like red-yellow ornaments. The smell is thick and lusty, the earth warm, strewn with mashed peaches.

We go to the college's induction that night at the Lutheran church where the sermon concerns temptation. "If it leads you astray, know that Jesus Christ is Lord, and it will help in a moment of indecision. If you are tempted to go to a party where beer is probably going to be served, and ugly, vulgar language is going to be spoken, remember: Jesus Christ is Lord and your decision will be easier to live with."

The Welcome Wagon lady welcomes me at my house with a yardstick (Winfield Lumber); a comb; matches; coupons for three lanes of free bowling; men's hose (Anthony's); a box of detergent (Sears' catalogue store); candy (Rexall's); a pound of bacon (Sheneman's Meat Mart); key chain (First National Bank of Winfield); more matches; $2.00 off dry cleaning; four loads of free wash; a promise that an insurance man will call; a gold Kansas state insignia; a 4-H information book; a free photo portrait; a free haircut.

Driving downtown I see everyone pulling over to stop, so I follow suit, having no idea why. I look for a fire truck and listen for a siren. What arrives instead is a funeral procession. The man in the pickup truck in front of me takes off his hat and waits until the last car goes by before pulling back onto the road. Winfield has time to acknowledge death.

I buy a twelve-dollar ticket to three days of bluegrass music in the fall. This year is the Fourth Annual Flatpicking Contest at the Walnut Valley Bluegrass Festival held at the fairgrounds. Over ten thousand people show up, a size close to Winfield's population. Most come from out of state, many camping. The atmosphere is dirty denim. As the flat pickers pick, the audience applauds appropriately, rewarding the great, acknowledging the fair. There are craft booths outside, under shelters, inside barns, and under the grandstand: leather boots and belts, make-it-yourself dulcimers, thrown pottery, handmade jewelry. In one barn, a banjo contest plucks its way through eighteen competing pickers. At night, the grandstand is full to hear Norman Blake and Dan Crary. The moon rises above them, a few clouds covering it to make the setting slightly mysterious. A Santa Fe freight passes a quarter mile away. As Ann says, it is a meeting of opposites: old and young, redneck and freak. The music matters; it centers everyone. The jeans, hats, sneakers, and boots are here for the tunes, a smorgasbord of bluegrass, 10 a.m. 'til midnight, three days straight.

I find living in a small town requires little or no thinking. Without the anxiety of an urban environment, happiness results with the comfort of security. Here is a place of belonging, where thinking has no place. Life here is set, stable, sure; the future does not include change. I feel it would be easy to remain here the rest of my life, and I am wary.

I begin asking myself if I like living in Paradise.

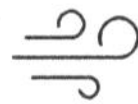

It is spring, and Ann is here. We want to go to the Winfield City Lake but are not sure where it is. We pull into an aging Mobil station that might have sold gas since the Depression. A man in dirty, green coveralls and visored cap plugs in the pump and wipes the windshield.

"You know the way to City Lake?" I ask out the driver's window.

"Yip " he says, continuing his slow, circular motion.

"You know which way we should go out of town?" I ask.

"Yip," he answers, moving to Ann's side of the windshield.

I lean across Ann. "Would you tell us how to get there?"

"Yip," he says, and does.

One's first sight of the lake surprises as a surrealist's painting surprises; it could be a mirage. In the middle of a pale, flat field, a three-mile-long puddle has risen from a river now dammed. A man drowned here, I'm told, pinned while taking his boat off the trailer, a feat analogous to dying of sunstroke in Antarctica. We swim over sand brought in from another state.

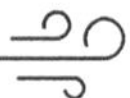

In May, the college president calls me into his office. The professor on sabbatical for whom I substituted is returning next year. There will be an opening for me if I agree to coach the basketball team, even though the last time I played organized basketball was in eighth-grade shirts and skins gym classes.

"I played hockey, not hoops," I tell him, knowing I'm getting myself fired.

As I leave his office and walk the block from the school back to my Winfield home, I'm walking away from the middle class: schedules, responsibility, and the comfort of being part of a community. I have relaxed this year, and I am not ready to leave. I am addicted to Winfield.

I'll have to go cold turkey.

The last four nights in Winfield I suffer nightmares. Daytime temperatures reach 94 degrees. The air conditioning cannot keep up, cannot lower the temperature in the house past 81, even at night. With plants on the windowsills, I cannot air out the house. Surrounded by long, green shoots and musty antiques, I myself feel old.

Then I am aloft again, without wing, without rudder.

A Focus of Enhancement

FRIDAY, January 23, 2015

Toward the end of second period, my cell phone rings, interrupting a class on American literature, most likely *Huckleberry Finn* and/or the basics of writing a short story, taught in tandem. Tia. I leave the classroom and stand next to the lockers.

"Are you in class?"

"Yeah, but it's okay. I'm in the hall."

She tells me her gynecologist, Dr. Hussey (I couldn't make that up), just called after reviewing the radiologist's report from Tia's mammogram taken earlier today. He told her he saw a tumor, but benign or cancerous was not discernable.

"He wants me to get a biopsy this afternoon."

A few weeks earlier, during a self-exam, Tia had felt a lump in her right breast. Hard, like a frozen pea, she said. At her appointment with Dr. Hussey two days ago, he'd also felt it.

"Want me to come over?" Delnor, a small, suburban, Northwestern Medicine hospital, was a few blocks from our house.

"No, it's okay."

We live in the Fox River Valley, an hour west of Chicago, on a quiet, middle-class street. Most people describe our hometown as "quaint," meaning it has a late Victorian vibe—cobblestone pedestrian crossings and faux gas lamps ornamenting the downtown shopping.

Later that day, my son Jay and I watch a recent *Justified* on the basement's 60-inch Samsung. I'm sitting on the floor, leaning back on the L-shaped couch where Jay is splayed out. He lives in a Chicago studio apartment and works for a large landscaping firm, so our time to bond over Marvel movies and spectacular TV is rare.

The land line rings and announces Tia. "How are you?" I ask.

"Not so good." Her voice sounds weary, distressed.

"What's going on?"

"I had just left school when the radiologist called. She asked where I was. I told her I was driving home. She asked could I pull over. After I stopped, she said Dr. Hussey did find something. He wants me to get an ultrasound as soon as possible."

My stomach knotted. A life in control, a life of routine, a sheltered life, starts to feel confused, unregulated, untenable. I cannot do anything about this. I feel adrift.

Once home, Tia hangs her purse on the basement doorknob and picks up Summer, our elderly rescue miniature poodle, ecstasy at seeing Tia shaking her body. "Maybe I should be more nervous, but I'm not," Tia confesses. "One percent of the time I panic."

After dinner, Tia and Jay watch *Guardians of the Galaxy* while I wash the dishes. In an opening scene, the hero's mother is in bed, dying.

"That's me," Tia says.

Jay and I can't help ourselves; we guffaw at her dark, hypberbolic, pessimistic humor.

Before bed, Tia shows me the x-rays. In the left breast, clean fog. In the right breast, looming out of the fog at twelve o'clock, a round dark spot. "One millimeter," Tia quotes her radiologist. "I teared up when they told me it was a tumor."

That morning, I had made an appointment to see the principal of the parochial single-sex (boys) secondary school where I taught English for 35 years. "I teared up when I told Tony."

"That's nice," Tia smiles.

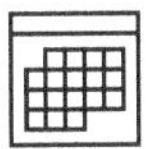

MONDAY, January 26

I call Tia on my way home from school. When she says "Hello?" I know there's news.

"Level one," she says, and I think that's good, but not sure. I haven't learned cancer yet. When I go upstairs to change out of my teaching clothes—khakis, button-down shirt, tie, jacket—I google the levels. Yes, one is good. Or at least better than two through four.

"It's 'stage' one, not 'level' one," Tia later corrects us.

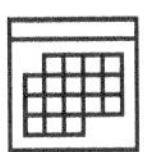

FRIDAY, January 30

At Delnor's Cancer Center, Dr. Mary Ahn, a surgical oncologist, preps Tia and me for her lumpectomy. She reminds me of Illinois Senator Tammy Duckworth, Asian-American, shoulder-length brown hair, John Lennon glasses. She puts us at ease, her soft, assuring, confident manner both nurturing and expert. I take notes. Someone has told me that for these appointments the cancer patient may be unaware of her trauma and will remember few of the details meted out. I, too, am traumatized, but taking notes in my journal grounds me. Later when I review what I've written:

Diagnosed with cancer
Take care of self
Family leave thing—can't take care with few days off—58 days to use
A—Found lump self?
T—No family history, nursed both children supposed to reduce cancer risk
A—Risk reduction of nursing tiny—just as many get cancer who didn't nurse
10 to 15 % have genetic history. Probably just bad luck—can't pinpoint—new chemicals, the air, food.
After lumpectomy, recoop minimum 2 weeks—4-7 days no teach—day 4 drive okay
2 to 3 days, path report—radiation appointments
No narcotic pain after day 2 usually—narco nite of surgery—next day Tylenol + 1 narco
Next day Tylenol only
Stage 1/Grade 1
1—slow, sluggish
3—aggressive
Staging—tumor size and lifetime prognosis
Likely, chemo <u>low</u>
After surgery—do things on own—but no laundry—no repetitive action
Walking with arm swings 90 degrees 1 week after surgery
Physical therapy—range of motion exs.
Right breast lumpectomy 2/12—surgery
23rd back to work
Dissolving stitches—gauze on 1 wk.—shower next day

Living Well—cancer resource center—free—massages, yoga—volunteers—tour—culinary classes—dieticians

In the meeting, Tia and I both sob, unable to bear even good cancer news stoically. A tissue box waits close to our chairs.

Next, we see Dr. Perry Menini, a specialist in hematology and oncology focusing on breast cancer, who resembles a mid-career Stanley Tucci with hair and a shadow beard. Again, from my journal:

M—right breast: hi density—very white—category 5—likely cancer—Grade 1 invasive ductile carcinoma
Grade 1—how fast cells growing—slowest growth
Good—estrogen 70-% progesterone 90%
Prognosis—less aggressive
KI67—gene—correlates to aggressive cancer—low

Again, tears from both of us even with Dr. Menini's reassuring "We'll get through this" bedside manner.

SUNDAY, February 1

"Grade 1" determined by the tests on Friday. Good news.

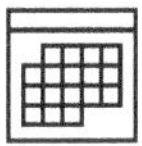

SUNDAY, February 8

In an upstairs bedroom, Jay and I watch *The Walking Dead.* Afterward, we find Tia at the kitchen sink polishing a silver tray and water pitcher.

“People are bringing dinner over. I need to clean,” she says. “The thing I’m most concerned about now is not the operation but the radiation. They say traditional, long-term radiation works better than the one-week. The first few weeks you don’t have any side effects, but it’s the last few that I’m worried about.”

Menini used the word “fatigued” to describe how she’ll feel.

> *“Right breast lumpectomy with intraopertive localization and sentinel node biopsy 2/12/15. Right breast, 1200/4NP, core biopsy for mass:*
> *Infiltrating ductal carcinoma, Grade 1, At least 0.5 cm.”*
> *“There is a focus of enhancement measuring 13X10X13 mm seen in the anterior region of the right breast, corresponding to the mammography lesion noted to be at the 12:00 position 4 cm from the nipple. The lesion demonstrates mixed kinetics with approximately 50% rapid and 50% medium uptake with predominant type I and type II curves.”*
> *“Procedure: Excision with wire-guided localization.*
> *Lymph Node Sampling: Sentinel lymph node.*
> *Histologic Type of Invasive Carcinoma: Invasive ductal carcinoma.”*

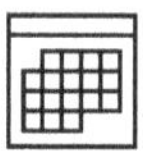

SATURDAY, February 14, Valentine's Day

After surgery, we drive home, thirty-mile-an-hour wind gusts willowing sheets of snow over the streets. Tia says the nuclear radioactive medical serum injected to find the lymph node hurt the most.

"It felt like a bee sting. A queen bee. It felt hot."

"Oooh," I grit my teeth.

"Dr. Ahn said she pulled things together and tightened things up. Darn. Wish she'd tightened things on my chin and throat, too."

At home, walking upstairs, Tia calls down, "All I can say is, this sure is better than a hysterectomy." She looks at her breast. "Not even stitches on top. Stitches inside. A Steri strip outside."

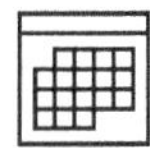

SATURDAY, February 15

Neighbor Jill and her mother, Marilyn, a widow (after her husband pulled out of a side street onto a two-lane blacktop, not seeing the car that T-boned them), bring over soup and bread and stay for a glass of wine.

"I never went to Living Well," says Marilyn, a five-year cancer survivor, about the building a block away offering free services to cancer patient survivors.

"Let's make it a date," I suggest. "We'll all go over together."

(Months later, Tia and I take the tour. We're impressed most with the wig display, replete with more hair styles and colors than Moira Schitt's Rosebud Motel room. We go to an evening cooking class where about twenty cancer survivors and their spouses sit at long tables. Tia feels self-conscious about not having had a more dire cancer experience, as every survivor she talks to is either on chemo or has had chemo, their stories more devastating than hers.)

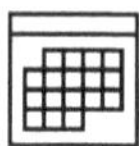

MONDAY, February 16, Presidents' Day

Tia's appointment with Menini to discuss the oncology report is Thursday morning, three long days from now. He calls to say he wants to wait until he sees Tia to go over it. When a doctor does not want to reveal information over the phone, one assumes bad news. Good news is easily and briefly relatable; bad news needs explanations, support, and reassurance.

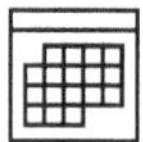

TUESDAY, February 17, Mardi Gras

Because Tia has a day off from teaching, I call home around 10:30 a.m., during my free period. When hearing the sadness in her voice, I ask, "What's going on?"

"Dr. Ahn called. She said they found cancer in the lymph node." I can tell she's crying. "I was so nervous I didn't write anything down, so I don't know what kind."

Tia and I talk about Ahn's rosy post-surgery report, leading us to anticipate a non-cancerous node. Since then, Tia has lived with that assumption. She has been led to expect the best and now is given news that indicates, probably, chemo. Which neither of us mentions. But we're both crushed, deflated, Tia's dream of radiation brutally sabotaged with the horrific nightmare of hair loss, vomiting, and an even deeper depression.

At home, I call Stephanie, a receptionist in the Alumni Office at school who had a mastectomy last summer. “Do you have time to talk to Tia?” I ask.

“I have all the time in the world.”

They talk for about an hour, Tia mostly listening and asking questions. After the call, Tia reports, “Stephanie said the chemo was really bad at first. Her hair hasn’t started growing back yet. She couldn’t go to work.” The solace and sympathy Stephanie offers I can see have helped Tia cope with an indeterminate future. The worst part of cancer for her and me so far, like flying through clouds, is knowing a mountain lies ahead, and not knowing if you will collide with it, get jounced by its mercurial uplifts and downdrafts, or somehow miraculously skirt it.

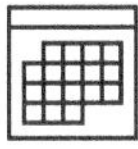

WEDNESDAY, February 18, Ash Wednesday

Driving to school this morning past the forest preserve on the other side of the road from Geneva’s windmill (brought over the Atlantic in pieces and sewn together before bought and erected across the Fox River from “Colonel” Fabyan’s home) I can see far into the woods. Naked of summer’s full, broad leaves and prickly undergrowth, the forest’s brown trunks and black branches spear skyward and sideways. On the ground, snow is packed in a hard, frozen, white nothingness.

Final surgical pathology report:

"Diagnosis:
A. Right axillary sentinel lymph node #1 for frozen section:
—lymph node with micro metastasis, 0.3 mm diameter
B. Right breast mass lumpectomy:
—Grade 2 moderately differentiated infiltrating ductal carcinoma of the breast (14 mm in greatest dimension)
—surgical margins of resection negative for tumor
—negative for vascular-lymphatic invasion"

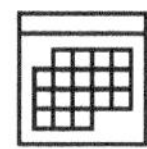

THURSDAY, February 19

After both the Menini and Ahn appointments (lots of statistics, but still no decision regarding radiation or chemotherapy), I shop our Meijer store: frozen fruit, navel oranges, McIntosh apples, Spring Mix lettuce, turkey sausages, coffee, decaf, eggs, birdseed, menthol cough drops, Duraflame logs.

FRIDAY, February 20

After school, lying on the family room couch, Tia says through tears, "It's at night that I break. I'm okay during the day."

I wake at 1:30 a.m. with night sweats and stay awake for hours. I worry about all the short stories still to read and grade; the poems, stories, essays, and chapter novels to critique for the two writing workshops I facilitate; the English 3

Honors' journals to evaluate; and our state and federal taxes to figure out.

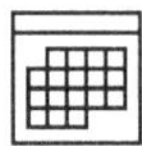

SUNDAY, February 22

Molly calls from Buffalo. I tell her I'm writing about Tia's cancer. "Is it weird...umm...that you're writing about...?"

Yes, I tell her. I've thought so, too. Am I somehow taking advantage of her sickness? I tell Molly (perhaps a rationalization) it's how I process stuff. I try to give the grotesque and draining situation some solemnity. Try to show its gravity. And its humor.

I tell her that I hope if my notes turn into an essay, it will help us remember someday what we forget so fast because it all happens so fast.

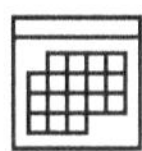

MONDAY, February 23

Before dinner, Jay asks Tia, "How was your first day back?"

"Great. All the kids were so sweet and cute."

"First time I've heard that," he laughs.

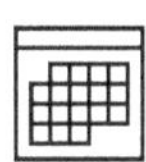

THURSDAY, March 5

Couldn't sleep past 3 a.m. so excited, manic, ecstatic that T's oncotype DX test results came back "low risk," meaning no chemo. Probably 4 weeks full breast & some underarm radiation, plus post-radiation hormonal therapy, a pill for 5-10 years.

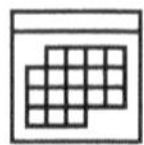

MONDAY, March 9

Tia's first appointment with radiation oncologist Kruser today.

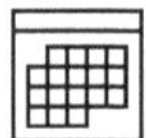

MONDAY, March 17

Tia goes to Living Well for a group meeting. Nedra leads the discussion. When Tia comes home, she looks stunned.

"The good thing is, I'm better off than everyone else there. Bad thing is they all told stories of it coming back. One woman now has cancer in her back. You can see it."

"Try to stick with the statistics and information Menini and Ahn are giving you."

"But they said once it's in you, it will come back. I don't think I'm going back. It's too dark and deep."

MONDAY, March 30

I can exhale again. Taxes are done (refunds!). Everything graded (until today when research papers come in).

SUNDAY, April 11, 2021

Six years later, I'm walking around our suburban block with Tia who holds Summer's leash. Cancer-free, Tia last year celebrated her five-year "graduation," a tradition, I learn, with cancer patients.

I tell Tia I wrote no journal entries recording her experiences with radiation. "Once I had that early morning manic awakening after hearing you wouldn't need chemo, I must have felt so relieved I stopped writing about your cancer." I say it as an apology.

"You weren't part of it," she says, perhaps at least partially excusing me. "I went there every day when you were still at school."

She reminds me of the process. "I'd go in, change into the robe they gave me, and go into the large room where they put on the lead vest before I lay on the bed. The pillow was shaped exactly to where they wanted my head. Then they lined up the machine that moved from right to left across my breast. The whole thing lasted about ten minutes."

She pauses, something bothering her. About halfway around the block of mostly identical homes except for front porches, garage door placement, and siding color and material, she asks if I would add something to the essay, something that has irritated her for six years.

Her school allows only seven personal days (including sickness) that faculty can take off with full pay. After that, for additional emergency days off, teachers receive 80 percent of their daily salary. After surgery, Tia took off several days to recover, Dr. Ahn's orders. Her absences were docked the 20 percent.

It wasn't the money, she assures me. Rather, the indignity, the lack of understanding, the dearth of compassion.

Cancer had cost much more than 20 percent.

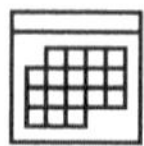

TUESDAY, May 26, 2015

Predawn:

I'm riding a bike with thick wheels down narrow lanes and along fences framing corn and soy fields. I wind up where Lake Shore Drive meets Sheridan Road. I need to take a bus, but I'm not sure of the fare.

"Three dollars," someone says.

I have 110-dollar bill, a 2-dollar bill, and a 1-dollar bill. The driver says he stops at the Drive and Burton Place, where I grew up.

We travel for hours. Going north on Michigan Avenue, the driver tells me to go into the Apple store to buy a travel-size toothpaste.

"It's dangerous," he says. I go in.

There are no windows in these carpeted rooms. Down two stairs I find a large bathroom. Inside a bureau with several drawers, I find clothes and travel-size items, but no toothpaste. I leave empty-handed and report to the bus driver that I couldn't find toothpaste. I have to get home.

We drive for a long time. We're back where we started, near a field. The driver tells me to calm down.

"Don't take life so seriously," he says. "Don't stress out."

I yell, "I have to get back!"

He says, "I'll be right back to drive the bus," and disappears into a large brick building. He appears in a second-floor window. He waves, pulls down the window shade, then rides up on it, as though ascending to a better place, and I know I'll never see him again.

Pallet Haven

"A word has power in and of itself....
By means of words can a man deal with
the world on equal terms."
~N. Scott Momaday,
The Way to Rainy Mountain

In 1971, after graduating from college, I set out to become a writer.

I bunked down on the foldout couch in the living room of my brother and sister-in-law's small cabin above a Walden-sized pond in North Branford, Connecticut. When not helping Bill dig out a basement room and throw in insulation, I read the classifieds and answered an ad for a cold storage grocery warehouse security guard. The interview offered minimum wage, $2.25/hour, eight-hour days/nights, five times a week.

"We may ask you to come in if we can't get anyone else," the HR person told me. "A guard might be sick. You might be asked to stay on the job for more than eight hours if your replacement is late or can't make it. Never leave your post unguarded. We'll get someone, but it might take time."

Sounded reasonable. After all, how long could they keep me hanging? Turned out, up to four hours.

"The warehouse needs 24-7 around-the-clock security. We're putting you on the 4:00 p.m. to midnight shift that a guard recently left."

HR didn't say why the guard left.

Finally, HR told me where to pick up my shirt, tie, and suit. I showed up next day at 3:30. A veteran guard, a lieutenant, showed me around. My stiff, black visored hat had a silver badge above the hard plastic rim; his was gold.

As for the warehouse, imagine everything you store in your refrigerator—or required refrigeration to stay fresh: produce, dairy, meat, OJ, even flowers. Now imagine a slightly smaller arena holding everything in your freezer: boxed veggies, potatoes, berries, sausages, pot pies. Ice.

At the rear of the building, beside a railroad track long enough to park two freight cars, wooden pallets towered higher than six feet. All day and night pallet jack drivers zoomed up a ramp into the cars, inserted the two protruding metal bars into a wooden pallet, lifted it up, zoomed down the ramp, and set them down on the platform. From there, forklifts, side loaders, walkie stackers, or reach fork trucks (depending on the product's destination—high on a shelf, side-by-side, etc.) deposited the merchandise on shelving as high as the highest lift allows. Once shelved, the merchandise waited for other forklift operators to pick up the pallets, roar over to the truck ports, and park the goods inside truck trailers that go to the company's retail stores.

The only retreat from the cold, besides the railroad platform (in warm weather), the maintenance department, was located at the rear of the freight car platform where Jack and Joe received workers who complained about malfunctioning machines—or dreamed up bogus mechanical problems as an excuse to warm up.

Once my tour guide left, I began walking the floor, skirting the rumbling, ubiquitous pallet jacks and stained yellow forklifts spewing blue exhaust. I didn't feel like an authority figure, but looked the part: the stiff, black hat, stiff, black wool uniform, stiff white shirt, and narrow black tie. I walked like I meant business, even though I had no idea what I was looking for, or what I'd do if I found it/them.

Before long, one of the relatively well-paid (compared to me), skilled warehouse workers roared up in his forklift. He wore a navy knit cap, denim coveralls, thick leather gloves, and steel-toed boots. His forklift idled and coughed smoke. He bent down.

"You the new guard?"

"Yeah!" I said, excited to make a friend.

"Know what happen to the old guard?"

"No."

"Quit. Know why?"

"No."

"Wrote up a worker for walking out with flowers for his old lady. Man got fired. That night, case of oranges fell off one of those top shelves." He pointed up. "Guard walking underneath when the box fell and damn near killed him. He was some lucky bastard. Guard left that night."

I might have thanked him for letting me know.

"All right." He sped off on his machine. I walked on. A few minutes later, another worker stopped.

"You the new guard?" he asked, and an identical dialogue repeated. I met many people that way that night. I knew enough to know I'd been threatened, knew enough to know what would happen if I did my job, knew enough that

I'd be run out with no warning, knew enough that I'd awakened to a life that, until then, I'd been insulated from.

From then on, I tried my best to avoid doing my job. I showed up, but other than that, I avoided that Arctic arena as long as I could, eluded the men and one or two women I was hired to keep track of, or prevent or deter them from stealing or choking on food belonging to the company. In other words, I flouted my duty to safeguard them and warehouse merchandise. From then on, and for the rest of my nine-month tenure, every afternoon when pushing open the swinging double rubber doors, I avoided my responsibilities in order to stay unthreatened, unhurt, and employed.

Like the warehouse workers, I, too, warmed up to the idea of thawing out in Maintenance, often taking advantage of the 75-degree, high-ceilinged room as large as a high school gym with shelves of tools and oil cans, and gray file cabinets stuck to vanilla walls. Jack, the head maintenance man, maybe in his late forties, had a smooth, calming voice and a face that could have sold men's cologne—and smelled like it. Joe, his assistant, a thin Black man who looked ten years older than Jack, would meet my arrival on Fridays by first asking what I was doing that weekend. I'd say something like driving to Oneonta to visit my girlfriend, still in college. In between his cackling laughter, he'd tell me he was "makin' babies, Richard, makin' babies." He already had nine children.

With my lousy bi-monthly check, I rented on the first floor of a brick house on Orange Street in New Haven a tiny apartment with two tiny rooms and a tiny bathroom separated from other living areas by thin wallboard. Leaving for work in the late afternoon and not returning home until after midnight worked for me, a morning writer. After work, before bed, around 1:00 a.m., I'd eat a cold hotdog or leftover hamburger from "dinner" eaten around 3:00 p.m.

After about seven or eight hours of sleep, I'd write three or four hours while drinking strong, caffeinated coffee perked in an old-fashioned coffee pot. My hands literally shook from a caffein high after five or six cups. I learned from Hemingway that a good place to stop for the day was when you know where the piece was going next, so you could pick it up easily from there the next day. Then I'd throw a burger in a pan or bake a chicken, shower, jump in the car, and it was 4:00 p.m., warehouse time.

After a month or two of walking officiously through the warehouse while looking the other way whenever anything untoward was spotted, I found a refuge, a sanctuary. Wandering the railroad dock, I discovered at the opposite end of the maintenance shop stood a stack of abandoned pallets about seven feet high. Standing behind this barrier, I escaped not only notice, but also time. I carried in my back pocket a worn paperback copy of Will Durant's *The Story of Philosophy*. Each chapter introduced a major philosopher and those who orbited him (always a him). Organized chronologically, the book began with Plato who, reading him, became the greatest thinker of all time until chapter two introduced Aristotle, who replaced Plato, and so on through William James. I had not the intelligence or background to critique such heady nuanced logic, values, and reasoning.

Reading Durant taught me not only the rudiments of philosophy but also offered a mottled vocabulary. For one anticipating the mantle of Great American Writer, my reading previous to Durant was laughably limited. Sure, I knew a few large, impressive words, but they came from reading the likes of H.P. Lovecraft and Bram Stoker.

In fact, the first short story I was busily churning out every morning, "The Observer," had as a protagonist a professional Observer living in a Chicago apartment building; he seeks out and collects lives observed through windows. He records the actions of those he watches on a complicated grid but never interferes, an objective correlative for the artist, recording life's events while revering the sanctity of their unfolding. The story's twist comes when he realizes someone is observing him. In the story's exciting climax, he tracks down the other Observer and, in case you haven't already guessed, *oh my gosh*, it turns out to be...*HIMSELF*!

I got the idea from growing up in a high-rise apartment building on Lake Shore Drive. My older brother, about ten at the time, with whom I shared a bedroom, took my father's binoculars from the living room where he watched sailboats and ore boats on Lake Michigan. They worked wonderfully for my brother inspecting tall condominium windows from our west-facing bedroom. One morning, he hit gold; reluctantly handing over the binoculars, he told me which window to focus on, and after a few minutes I caught sight of my first man and woman enjoying breakfast in front of a picture window in the nude.

To illustrate my naivete and ignorance, I looked forward to my first acceptance from a major magazine by sending "The Observer" to *Esquire*. A few months later, the inevitable rejection form (only slightly larger than a Chinese fortune cookie) arrived in my self-addressed stamped envelope. Below the formal text sent to all rejected manuscripts, a handwritten note was scrawled, "I like the plot, but the telling leaves me cold."

I needed to work on my diction, my style. I needed to be *au currant.*

As a start, behind my pallet tower, I took to circling, then jotting down inside the book's back cover, unfamiliar words. Next morning, I'd look up the definitions, and that night I'd read the words again in context. They became mine.

With a hideout and literary distraction, the eight, or sometimes ten or twelve hours (the nights my relief didn't show at midnight) became, if not enjoyable, at least less long and boring. Every two hours, I'd leave Schopenhauer or Kant or Voltaire and wander through the warehouse, smiling stupidly at workers who regarded me as their enemy. For good reason. They were stealing. They were eating and drinking a good deal of the boxed or bottled or crated food they were paid to move from refrigerated freight cars to shelves to trucks.

How did I know? After all, I never saw anyone consuming food. Circumstantial evidence. A truck bay light with an intensely bright bulb screwed into a round metal canister supposed to be aimed into a trailer's dark interior would be pointed not horizontally, but vertically, at the ceiling; nesting on the bulb's scalding surface sat an unboxed, silver-tinned, chicken (or turkey) pot pie. Elsewhere, a sink into which boiling water ran was heating a ten-pack of Oscar Meyer All-Meat Wieners. Discarded milk cartons, orange juice bottles, and yogurt cups littered the floors like back-alley trash day.

Always, I looked the other way. Why write a worker up and get him fired and have his life changed forever for guzzling a quart of 2% milk?

Besides, I wanted to be liked. I wanted the workers to recognize me as a person, not a uniform. I was an impoverished writer, damn it, working my ass off just to get by, just like them.

One night a pallet jack rumbled past, and I waved my hand. "Hey, buddy."

The machine jerked to a stop. "I ain't your buddy," the man scowled, then accelerated away with an ascending wheeeEEEEE of his electric motor.

So much for camaraderie.

After three or four months, I learned that guards were requested, when called, to go to the company office to take a polygraph test. Legally, our company could not force anyone to undergo the nerve-racking ordeal and could not fire a guard for not complying. However, the guards' grapevine told me that one person who refused to go in was harassed by the managers with "anonymous" phone calls throughout the night. He eventually quit—or was fired—for a minor infraction.

Driving to my appointment, I foresaw that after a day or two I'd be fired for any number of infractions: occasionally napping around 1:00 a.m. if my replacement hadn't arrived; for not being diligent in looking for and acting on employee offenses; for reading philosophy when I should have been searching out chicken pot pie and all-meat wiener gourmands.

In a small, windowless room, the examiner hooked me up with a coiled something-or-other across my chest, another coil wrapped around my arm, and something hooked onto a finger. After asking a few baseline questions (name, address, birthday, etc.), he started in on getting the dirt.

"Have you ever slept on the job?"

I confessed, yes, a short nap now and then when I could no longer keep my eyes open.

"Have you ever stolen anything?"

No, I was clean.

He posed a few more incisive questions, but those are the two I remember. Nothing about reading, though. I felt exonerated.

A few minutes later, he told me the test was over and started futzing with dials and jotting things on a sheet of paper. "So," he asked offhandedly, "what do you do when you're not at work?"

"Oh," I brightened, eager to relay my passion, "I write. I'm a writer."

"What do you write?" He was all ears, fascinated.

"Short stories right now. But I'm thinking about starting a novel," I began, then jabbered for another few minutes.

"So, if you're a writer, you must like to read."

"Yeah!" I said, excited to let him in on my favorite authors and books—before realizing what I'd just confessed to. Instantly hot, I felt sweat bead my forehead.

"Ever read on the job?" he said as though he couldn't care less.

I was still hooked up. I couldn't see the needle, didn't know if it was registering my pulse and anything else accelerating, but his question suggested something more than a personal interest. I couldn't lie. "Uh-huh."

"How much? Fifteen minutes?"

"Yeah," I confirmed.

"More? Half an hour?"

"Sometimes."

"An hour?"

"Well, yeah."

"Two hours?" His voice rose in what might have been incredulity, if not disbelief.

"Occasionally."

"Three hours? Four?"

"Maybe four. Now and again."

I don't remember how long his interrogation, this waterboarding continued. All I remember is leaving the office convinced I'd get a call from my boss, the lieutenant at the main warehouse, telling me I was fired for reading on the job.

It never came. Apparently, literature was overlooked as a vice. Just don't steal a package of bacon.

About five months into my tour of duty, the warehouse lieutenant sent a memo telling us guards (three additional guards were stationed in the main—much warmer and larger—warehouse) to flesh out our daily reports. When first joining the firm, I'd been schooled to write something short, neutral, and inane like, "Patrolled the warehouse, all secure." The lieutenant now made it clear he wanted a more detailed description of our activities, perhaps even describing any anomalies observed, evidence that employees had been enjoying the fruits, literally, of their labor. If I started ratting them out, however, their bosses and my bosses would most likely move in on the culprits, look for those working such and such an area where chicken pot pies warmed, perhaps making me do stakeouts resulting in an orange crate crushing my head.

No, I couldn't rat out hungry warehouse workers. Wouldn't. But I could improve my report in another way.

Asking for lengthier reports offered an opportunity for putting my newly acquired lexicon to good use. All those big words just waiting to burst upon the blank page of a daily report! Oh, how my new multi-syllabic concordance would impress the lieutenant! I began that night employing gargantuan nomenclature, journalistically rendering my perambulations and circumlocutions of expostulated premises, devising titanic diction and multifaceted verbiage, proliferating the superfluous and/or redundant potential to engage in the superlative and hyperbolic verbosity of linguistic bullshit.

My daily reports turned out to be, in my mind, masterpieces of turgid claptrap. I had so much fun writing them, I often ran out of space on the ten-by-twelve-inch form and continued to drip my dreck on the back. No one ever had more fun writing purple prose.

After two or three weeks of submitting these masterpieces of glib gibberish, I received a call at home. Someone asked me my name, after which the company lieutenant introduced himself and said, "I wonder if you'd stop by my office this afternoon for a few minutes before you go on duty."

When I hung up, my stomach hurt. I stood frozen, staring straight ahead at nothing. I was going to be fired for being a literary smartass. Not that I liked the job all that much, but I'd tamed it, could live with it. A known routine was better than being uprooted and tossed into the jobless compost heap.

The lieutenant's office was in the main warehouse, resplendent with gray metal chairs, desk, file cabinets, and walls. His uniform, like mine, was black; unlike mine, it was spotless. He invited me to sit down.

A pile of daily reports sat on the desk in front of him. I recognized my handwriting. I sat silently as he paged through them. I studied his face, a handsome, rock-like, forty-something actor's facade, topped off with short, curly, black hair.

He picked up the top report, held it out to me. "Did you write this?"

I took it, and even though I didn't need to, read it like my obituary. The first few lines revealed it as one of my finest achievements, blather about absolutely nothing I'd done that night except write a delightfully obscure description of my efforts to look like I'd been productive and efficient in my job while accomplishing the opposite.

"Yes, sir," I answered and handed it back, certain that tomorrow I'd be back with other losers sitting in front of a Cutco HR slicing "rope beef," or a Rainbow vacuum HR selling a new, futuristic, "environmental-friendly" device.

The lieutenant looked rigid as a paperweight as he focused on the report I'd just handed back. Finally, he looked up.

"How would you like to be a lieutenant?"

Huh? A what? A lieutenant? Not a pink-slipped security guard?

"The position pays a dollar more," he continued. "Three-twenty-five an hour. A dollar more than you're making now."

Not being a math genius but having learned something in Mrs. Kramer's third grade class, I figured something in the vicinity of a 33% raise. However, stunned at the thought of losing Pallet Haven, I asked, "What would I have to do?"

"You'd be stationed at the entrance of the main warehouse. You'd check people in and out. You'd also call for replacements when a guard calls in sick."

No more hiding behind stacked pallets? No more gleaning the masterminds of philosophy, accumulating the ontological and epistemological differences between a Kierkegaard and Comte? No more vocabulary building? No way.

"Um, I like being a guard, sir."

He looked at me as if I'd just turned down a piece of his wife's homemade apple pie with a scoop of cinnamon ice cream. Turn down a promotion of rank along with a phenomenal pay raise? Turn up your nose at a shiny *gold* badge? Reject without reflection an office as self-important as his? Unbelievable.

It threw a burning flag in the face of the American Dream.

The lieutenant told me to think about it, so I did. Next day, I called him and formally declined his offer. I couldn't give up my safe harbor, my reading space, my pallet haven. The new position would have meant high visibility, sitting in a Plexiglass booth like a Nuremburg prisoner while pleading with guards to take extended shifts or to come in on their day off, making me their enemy. It meant real responsibility.

The interview with the lieutenant, however, taught me a valuable lesson: words count. I would have jumped two ranks (leapfrogging sergeant) and earned a salary beyond my wildest expectations, simply by writing texts that fooled the lieutenant into believing me sophisticated, scholarly, and/or proficient. Maybe I could pass for above average for some of his expectations, but the fact that he mistook bluster and bullshit for erudite, lyrical, inspired prose, well, that's on him.

Up until then, I loved using words, but had no idea of their true potential, no idea of how both dangerous and sublime they might prove. The lieutenant's offer of promotion, even though turned down, illuminated both the volatile and nurturing nature of words.

That morning, after giving the lieutenant my answer, for the first time, I began to write like my life, and life in general, depended on it.

Wonders to Behold When Growing Old

I'm back in the North Woods. I look out the window above this desk made of three pine boards and see a forest of long-needle white pines, short-needle firs, brawny red pines, and a few scraggly maples street fighting their way up.

Looking south, I find the sun rising over an azure lake brushed with white mist. Near shore, a feeding largemouth bass sends out a ring of wavelets. I hear overhead the high-pitched squeak of an immature eagle.

Yesterday, I took a short walk. Short, because less than a quarter mile away, down a grassy path, a momma black bear and her cub visited the trout pond where I often fly fish.

On my walk, I discovered what passed for splendor:

> A grouping of what looked like a triad of blueberries.
>
> A gray leaf pockmarked with droplets from morning rain.

A bell-shaped blossom neither blue nor purple but could have been either.

A monarch butterfly flitting from leaf to leaf as if each were hot to the touch.

A small creek whose sandy bottom glowed in the dappled afternoon sun like golden granules.

A grove of quaking aspen, their leaves flirting with the breeze, and tea-green leaves fluttering like wispy butterfly wings.

I am moved by what to my younger self would have been taken for granted—or ignored. I am older now.

Older than days filled with dart gun fights, water balloon battles, cannonball contests, fishing ventures, numerous walks in and out of the woods (some call it golf).

Older than when emotions boomeranged between ecstasy and distress depending on the look a girl gave me when asked if she wanted to crew for me in a sailboat race.

On whether or not I landed the northern pike stuck in a weed bed ten feet deep.

On being tagged and jailed or winning the game by kicking the can.

On having two dimes to buy the latest Superman and Beetle Bailey comic books.

On making it back to the cabin after a walk around the lake with or without ticks, bulbous with blood, burrowed into my skin.

On hearing my father tell my brothers and me we were going logging to chop down dead trees, cut them up with a two-man saw into four-foot lengths and then quarter them with sledge and wedges into fireplace logs—or be asked by friends to serve as a fourth for tennis.

Youth favors action. A septuagenarian, I've left action—except for physical therapy exercises, occasional trips to the gym, and half-hour walks along public wooded trails.

Instead, I'm drawn to nature.

In 1856, on a cold night in Dixon, Illinois, Ralph Waldo Emerson delivered a lecture defining "beauty" as "the moment of transition, as if the form were just ready to flow into other forms." In a word, flux.

"The feat of the imagination is in showing the convertibility of every thing into every other thing.... My boots and chair and candlestick are fairies in disguise, meteors and constellations."

When I look at a sunflower eyeing its namesake, or I stumble across a newborn fawn lying curled asleep, I am moved beyond the artless notion of identifying the physical forms of a flower and deer.

On her June 23rd podcast "The Happiness Lab," Dr. Laurie Santos recommends we become more attuned to moments in life that deliver a sense of wonder, awe. Some find revelation in religious devotion; others, like me, find, as did the Romantic poet William Blake, "...a World in a Grain of Sand / And a Heaven in a Wild Flower."

The Best Friend of Writers and Artists

Entering a big box hardware store, I knew exactly what I wanted: a Kohler Elliston Rev 360 EB White Elongated Bowl with AquaPiston POWER Behind the Flush, Slow-close Seat Included.

After a half mile walk, I saw underneath "Bath" and "Plumbing" banners a man wearing a vest and nametag. Thinking I'd save time finding my desired product, I told Bob, "I'm looking for the toilets."

He looked at me with a curious expression. "The men's room is right over there."

"No, I want the TOILETS," I explained.

Exasperated, Bob spoke as if addressing a three-year-old. "Right. See the sign for the restrooms? They are under it."

"No! Where are your *toilets*?!"

Bob, now foaming at the mouth, yelled something into his walkie talkie and soon reinforcements arrived, but I was finished with this hardware store version of "Who's on First?", so I said, "I Don't Know's on third" and headed off to find the toilets myself.

The interaction may not have happened exactly that way, but I finally found my toilet, and, given how much Bob had sacrificed in time and sanity, I ordered not one, but two Kohlers.

Sometimes I wonder if I'm really suited to be a writer when finding it so difficult to make myself understood. I mean, it's what I love to do; every morning I either write in my journal or throw down a few fictional sentences or poetic lines and tell myself, "Good job, Rick!" as if I'd just renovated Versailles or touched up the Mona Lisa's smile.

On reflection, the most important aspect of my life that keeps me writing may be my personality. I'm rather a cynic, or, perhaps more accurate, a pessimist, which means, in my mind, a realist. Whether writing stories, essays, or poetry, the essential ingredient to getting it written, then read, is stirring in a couple of potent—yet nontoxic—teaspoons of conflict.

Which creates tension.

Which writers need to live—or, at least, recognize or intuit—to have their words be believed and read when writing about emotions. Like getting frustrated when hunting down toilets.

Poet John Keats called this "negative capability," the ability of artists to fully imagine a wide range of feelings and attitudes without necessarily having personally experienced them. Shakespeare, indubitably, mastered this better than any other author, imagining fully rounded characters from male to female, rich to impoverished, witty to witless.

Do I have an ounce of what Shakespeare had a pound of? Surely one needs to be part voyeur of human nature and part participant. The artist lives both inside and outside the norm, observing and indulging.

But doesn't everyone at some time believe, or at least entertain the thought, that they are living a singular life, and everything else is a dream—or nonexistent?

No? Hmm.

Reading Will Dowd's marvelous book of essays, *Areas of Fog*, I loved his recounting of getting drunk with a James Joyce scholar who, hearing Dowd was an aspiring writer, asked, "Sure you're neurotic enough?"

Creativity scholar Dean Simonton reminds us Plato believed "'the sane mind knocks in vain at the door of poetry' and Aristotle [claimed] 'no great genius has ever existed without some touch of madness.'"

From Dictionary.com, "Neurosis: a mental condition...involving symptoms of stress (depression, anxiety, obsessive behavior) but not a radical loss of touch with reality."

Good to know that as depressed, anxious, and/or obsessive artists may be, they're still tethered to reality.

You are out there, aren't you reader?

Manure Dreams 140

An Essay on Distrac—What? Huh? Where Was I Going with This?

Now retired from teaching, floating lazily through my *mature* (I love euphemisms) years, I find my friends have, somehow, inexplicably, also grown older. Our discussions over breakfast, lunch, or 4:00 o'clock dinners fascinate because our experiences mirror each other. In addition, our elderly "transitions" are not dangerous, but rather endearing, loveable.

Our loved ones, however, find our flaws frustrating, especially when we arrive late, forget to pick up the one thing they ask us to buy (Tabasco sauce), or request five minutes on a tech problem that takes three hours.

A common problem can be illustrated thus: I'm going from kitchen to bedroom to grab something; upon arrival, I look around the room as if I having wandered into the bedroom at the end of *2001: A Space Odyssey*. It's not until I return to the kitchen, spot the full pot of coffee, do I remember the coffee mug on my desk.

Hang on a second. Gotta check my Facebook posts.

Okay, I'm back. Never enough "Likes," but you learn to live with the ones you get, especially if there's a heart or crying-happy face.

Now, what was I talking about? Oh, right, becoming distracted by a text DINNNGGGG, a phone's RINNNNGGGG, or the spouse's question from one floor and three rooms away.

So how can we focus better?

One idea arrived in a book assigned to a new group of poets corralled at the Batavia Library. Kim Addonizio, in *Ordinary Genius*, to silence a multitude of voices and screens, suggests, "Sit still for a moment. It doesn't need to be a long moment; a few deep breaths, enough to clear your head and center yourself."

Poet Billy Collins expounds on this in "I Ask You":

What scene would I want
to be enveloped in
more than this one,
an ordinary night at the kitchen table,
floral wallpaper pressing in,
white cabinets full of glass
the telephone silent,
a pen tilted back in my hand.

Sorry, be right back. It's been five minutes since I checked my email.

Okay, got my forty-eighth dopamine hit of the day.

Where was I? Oh, right. How to maintain attention despite distractions.

In *Aflame*, Pico Iyer's memoir of his visitation to a Benedictine monastery above California's Big Sur, he learns about and practices quietude. Once, when leaving the mountain, he tells a friend about his new home, including,

> "The fact there's no need of texts or theories. It's just silence and emptiness and light. No screens at all."
>
> "No screens,'" his friend repeats, understanding Iyer means nothing other than than television sets.

In a TED talk, Iyer elaborates: "...going nowhere was at least as exciting as going to Tibet or to Cuba... . I mean nothing more intimidating than...to sit still long enough to find out what moves you most, to recall where your truest happiness lies."

In Mark Haber's novel, *Lesser Ruins*, a community college teacher is bent on writing about his hero, Michel de Montaigne, but is plagued by interruptions:

> I yearned for the time to...do the slow thinking banished from our contemporary world," he muses, "impervious to...half-baked howls and shrieks, rants and inanities, in short, our world's *incoherence*.

Henry David Thoreau is famous in his work *Walden* for dodging distractions, taking off for the woods, not to play hermit, but "to live deliberately, to front only the essential facts of life." We don't need a forest; we need only to "not be thrown off the track by every nutshell and mosquito's wing that falls on the rails."

Oops, there's the doorbell. Must be Amazon. Be right back.

Teacher Shortage: Love's Labor Lost

With Labor Day coming up, I've been thinking about labor. Or, actually, the dearth of labor. According to a recent Rand Corp. survey in 2021, in 2020, almost 1 in 4 teachers said they may leave their job.

Why? According to *Capitol News Illinois*, "for a variety of reasons, including the cost of a college education and the salaries teachers earn after graduating, teaching has become a less attractive career."

Occasionally, someone will quote this dictum: "Teachers don't teach for the income. They teach for the outcome." The idea infuriates me. The nefarious subtext suggests that the only compensation teachers need is their saintly passion for passing on knowledge.

The naïve reader concludes, "If teachers love what they do, why pay them anything more than mere subsistence?"

Those deluded folks need to absorb this statistic: "A strong correlation exists between the severity of the shortage and the average teacher salary in a given district. As teacher salaries increase, superintendents report less of a problem with shortages."

Every colleague I've known while teaching in high school, community college, and university classrooms, besides being passionate and well-versed in her subject, likes to earn enough money to spend, to save, and, occasionally, to splurge. The minimum 2021 teacher's salary of about $34,000, to graduates with student debt draining thousands, sounds paltry compared to enticing salaries of private corporate and tech companies.

Oh, wait, I forgot. The teacher *loves* her outcome, so living in a cramped studio apartment with noisy radiators, noisy neighbors, and silent air conditioning because there is none doesn't matter.

Be assured, I'm not belittling the "outcome," the moments teachers find they made an impact on a student, maybe fired them up to write a novel, or major in anthropology after an inspiring discussion of Margaret Mead's heroics. I, too, am genuinely moved when hearing about such an outcome.

James Joseph, owner of The Book Shop Batavia, wrote on Facebook recently, "A friend came into the shop, and we got to talking about the impressive book collection. I said there was about to be an even more impressive collection. I told him I helped Dr. Holinger downsize, and the shop would be stocking his remarkable collection of literature, poetry, and philosophy. My friend remembered Doc from Marmion Academy and vividly remembered his passion for poetry and literature. He said how fitting it was that his former teacher's books would be in my shop.

"I've been trying to figure out what else I can do with what matters so much to me. Hearing another story about a teacher having a profound influence on someone has settled my mind.

"Now, where do I sign up?"

Thank you, James, for your story. If passion for one's subject trumps everything else, a strong background in one's subject area is the ace of spades—and your love of reading suits you perfectly for teaching English.

When visiting James's shop, 15 N. River St., (847) 337-3876, pick up one or two of my former books, maybe even one that I read, and enjoy cryptic marginalia, like "Wow!" or "God?"

You might even find some title pages signed by their authors; instead of donating them to a library or museum, I offered them to James. The book couldn't land in better hands than his—or yours.

Reading these books, or any book, however, you might reflect on what went into writing them. The author first was taught how to read by a teacher, had read books by authors inspired by educators, and had worked with dedicated editors and publishers to put the books together.

Teachers live an intensive labor of rising 180 days of the year, often before dawn, commuting to school, walking into a classroom, and delivering with a passion and dedication their students may not appreciate, but will revere, maybe not then, not even at recess, but someday, maybe when they, too, understand what commitment to a dream means.

A Map of the Beautiful

A Map of the Beautiful, Part One

Outside these picture windows, Jay, my son, 34, works hard. A landscaper landscaping his 2.5 acres, Jay bought this house on a hill an hour and a half west of Chicago overlooking a muddy lake with carp, bass, and panfish. He catches them all, but with unequal passion. His mother and I are planted inside, invited by Jay until we finish renovations on the house next door that a widow sold us when, we believe, enough mouse shit peppered her couches, chairs, and beds.

Jay lifts his hydraulic trailer, the "Ultimate Dump." Out pours uprooted refuse from a client's yard they've paid to get rid of before replaced with what Jay has designed, printed, and presented in person, a map of the beautiful—arborvitaes, perennials, hardscape deck, water feature, pebbled runoff slough, and mulch, much mulch, a bunch of mulch, because mulch is beautiful, too, smothering the unwanted, burying the varied, eclipsing the ravenous, condemning the random so that those plants, shrubs, and trees on paper will blossom, spread, and grow tall as can be expected when first conceived in pixelated perfection in four-color 3-D.

I want a map of the beautiful, too. Each morning I would take Jay's map out of a lacquered cabinet, unroll it across the floor, and follow its daily insinuations to get a lay of the daily land: who to invite for eggs at Briana's Pancake House, what time to take for polishing a fiction or inventing a rhyme, and how far to go on walks through prairie flowers where Jerusalem Artichoke stretch as tall as when Lewis and Clark bit into its tubers, Hidatsa cooked, boiled over future North Dakota timber until soft and irreducible as a potato.

At day's end, I'd roll up the plan and place it back inside its home, lie down, and dream of what the next day's map will foretell, more heartache, disappointment, rejection, or the off chance of a miracle, like seeing a pileated woodpecker flutter its black and white wings onto the corn and seed brick feeder.

Weeding for Words

My son has asked me to weed his tomato plants. They grow along the rear of his house. I'm 75 and don't like to bend over. I drop a grape or pencil, and I look at it like I would stare down a toddler of five giving me the finger.

Because Jay is hosting my wife and me in his house until the renovation on our house next door is finished, I comply, put on my rattiest running shoes, some old Asics, and face the first row of caged plants. I have nothing against Jay's enemy, tiny sprouts fighting for air and sun, impervious to the reason for this deathbed scene—that they impinge on our love of beefsteak tomatoes. Whatever these tiny green stalks are, they're innocent of what they're being punished for. It's their bad luck that humans have an urge to feed themselves, keep themselves upright, and have returned to a desire for homegrown to feed on.

Walking row after row, stooping to tug up what's not planned, I go back inside, sit at my desk, and—from a mind three-quarters of a century old—pull words, their roots strong, holding them down, unwilling to give themselves up to whimsy, to anyone with gloves too dirty, with fingers too feeble.

Aristotle's Mean

Jay asked me to water the plants he installed last week, those vulnerable to heat, to drought, to neglect. He bought new sprinklers, state-of-the-spray, governing the amount of water released, and directing the liquid arcs' rotation and reach.

"We don't want water on the house's siding or foundation," he says, insinuating I know the water will turn the gray exteriors yellow, the color that the saline tablets in the water softener cannot correct.

Unpacking the first sprinkler, I'm impressed with its clever yellow levers, red rods, and blue disks. The contraption looks intimidating; I have to turn it on before I can adjust its spray, meaning I will get wet, no matter how far away I point the tiny parallel barrels. Trying to overcompensate, I set each setting on minimal spray—breadth and flow. I plant it in front of an island of blooming perennials and slowly turn on the spigot.

Slowly, silver slivers spit, stutter, then arc heroically above the mulched flowers, well within safe expulsion limits, far from the house.

Back and forth.

Back and forth.

Given this range, to moisten all the archipelagoed plots around the house will take not hours, but days, so, the water still gushing its miniature geysers, I push levers, turn disks, and twist rods, soaking my shorts, shirt, and shoes before returning it to where it levied water sparingly and watch it happily ejaculate over the gray concrete deck my son has ordered stay dry and gray. Feeling guilty, again sprinkler in hand, I push, turn, and twist the flow down, reminding me of Aristotle's practical Golden Mean, admittedly also my go-to position necessary in the inevitable fall of life after summering through the narcotic of middle age, content, I suppose, with moving the sprinkler as often as needed without abusing the walls or foundation needed to live in.

Meting Out the Law

Today Jay has invited his clients to gather at two of his landscaped homes to give a class in design and installation. It's sunny, hot, and humid, the start of August. We are still in the grip of a climate catastrophe causing Caribbean and Gulf hurricanes to shove saltwater waves onto and over beaches slowly but certainly disappearing; western forest fires as large as small states are leaving black all that's green; and blackouts and brownouts shade towns and cities where reservoirs run dry as desert dunes.

He's asked me to buy ice at the local Shell for three coolers filled with bottled water, beer, and lemon-flavored, unsweetened tea, respectively.

I tell him, if it's too hot by one o'clock when bringing folks back here, he's welcome to come inside and bring his disciples with. I've vacuumed the floors, put away washed dishes and clothes, even closed the doors to bedrooms whose sights should go unseen.

I leave out purposely the 1883 replica pellet pistol he gave me, laid it on the table just inside the front door to let his visitors know that someone metes out law and order in this house, inside and out, but they are, as well as I, especially I, am not clear who.

Plow

Shiny, black. "Forty-eight Inch." Today, when the temps will hit the upper 80s with a comfort index in the 90s, it sits, crated, in the pebble driveway waiting for winter, eager as an Alaskan husky.

One glance at the plow puts me in Jay's Bobcat's driver's seat, wool hat, scarf, down jacket, insulated pants, and fur-lined boots. Last night's blizzard blanched the earth like a cocaine dream. I turn the key, and the silent, sleeping land rumbles awake, the chained, knobbed tires claw forward, the plow aslant, its touch oddly incidental as it finds resistance minimal, the fallen surface pile as light as seeded dandelion globes.

The plow peels around the driveway and parking area clearing paths for two black pickups saddled to hulking, black, dump trailers; pushes clean the entrances to the storage shed and detached garage; drives snowdrifts into snowdrifts mountaining above me.

This Romantic waking dream melts in time, the summer sun returns with its relentless heat, the humidity mosquito thick, sunblock sprayed on every flesh surface like a fire hose dousing the least smoking ember.

Trap

Six cans of cat food stack along the kitchen counter. Outside—on the hardscape walk my son the landscaper has hammered in place, each brick a word in a novel never to be revised—sit three new, shiny, metal Havahart traps, mouths open, waiting to be baited, entered, and filled with who knows what—possum, woodchuck, skunk.

Eaters of wood ticks, mice, snakes, and other critters I'd rather not encounter, possums we let go.

And skunks, well, the smell is hell, so freeing a frightened, trapped skunk is delicate business. But free them we do, as they feed on snakes, cockroaches, mice, and, if in your neighborhood, black widow spiders. The downside is their taste for honeybees, the hive in Jay's woods a daily brunch buffet.

No, it's the chucks we're after. A.K.A. groundhogs. A.K.A. thick wood badger, moonack, land beaver, and whistling pig. One online site cites Spring Harbinger Chuck, apparently due to its seasonal Punxsutawney Phil Groundhog Day prediction. Another site refers to "SunScryer," a nod to chucks admiring their shadow.

Chucks can eat through wood foundations, nest inside sheltering sheds, shit indiscriminately—without the promise of flush—and generally disturb with the alacrity of a tornado what order has been imposed. These tendencies are a problem for a landscaper who capitalizes on color coordination; formal layout hinting at natural chaos; and non-incidentals like runoff, weed control, and soil enrichment; who invests richly in shears, clippers, spades, rakes, sledges, posthole diggers, blowers, chainsaws, etc., etc.; who shelves equipment and tools according to some mystic measurement dreamed either at night when random roaming conjures creativity, or when pushing down a shovel's lip with mud-caked boot, the earth's disruption shaking up his imagination better than an earthquake.

I slip an open tuna cat food can inside the trap. Next morning, I find a furry, white possum, apparently its stomach full, in a fetal curl. Wakening at my approach through tangled vines, wisteria, and thorny wild rosebushes, the possum opens its mouth to show off teeth tiny as clipped fingernails. When I open the door and tip up the cage, it balks, inhibited, more afraid of what awaits it outside the prison than the empty cat food shell and quiet reserve lasting the long night.

I walk away, giving it space and time to gather its wits. Tomorrow I'll return with another can of cat food and try again for a chuck. There will always be another chuck, even though we tell ourselves there's a sweet spot between eradicating all the chucks now here and the lure of others outside the territory by the sweet scent of the bait pulling more in.

Rider

The grass needs mowing, one of Frost's favorite tropes, his persona ogling blades, putting an ear to *swoosh* of scythe—and Whitman's titular *Leaves*, long green blades dotingly gazed at under his poetic microscope.

I'm more macro than micro, regarding the wide and steep expanse of hill my son's rider mower—handlebars for speed and turn and stop—runs up and down each week (or two, now that summer heat has parched spring's deluge). But once again, I've come too late, each pass leaving a wake spit out by cacophonous blades, hay-mown lines rippling the field like long, amber, prairie waves.

New technology, for all its added ease and speed, supplants the audible gift of *swishing* handheld blade or *clanking* curvaceous rotary push mower. Today, earbuds deaden motor roar and steel gyration, implanting instead Pandora or Spotify to mow the space between my ears and plug my soul with memories swirling like Fred and Ginger orchestrating space. I'm here but not here, suspended between past and present, riding above and shutting out the gift of mown grass, dandelions, windblown twigs, and who knows what flying and crawling insects whiplashed within tornadic whirl.

I could go back, drive to a farm estate sale and pick up a rusty, wood-handled push mower with blades bookended by long, woven grasses paled by time. I'd 3-in-1 oil it, use a gray metal file (my father once used to smooth birdhouse sides, roof and floor) to shine and sharpen the blades, then start downhill, green confetti flying out the top of the mower's swirling whir, soft as a kitten's purr.

But I won't. I'm addicted to saving time, to completing the job—any job—as a *job*, as fast as mechanically possible, not treating this event, this encounter with the natural world, as a Zen master would, as a means to understand myself in relation to the grass, the earth, the lives I'm taking (including each guillotined blade); as a means to slow down, to lounge; as a means to fulfill instead of expire.

And for that, I am less than I should be.

A Map of the Beautiful, Part Two

Writing this essay, I have found a Map of the Beautiful, as much inherent in plants, lawns, bees, sprinklers, blossoms, and woods, as much or more in my mind.

An analogy: My daughter, Molly, refuses to use the Rand McNally hard copy, spiral bound, collection of state maps my wife gave her for Christmas a decade ago. When traveling, she relies only on her cell phone.

"What happens," my wife asks, "if you can't get a signal when you're lost?"

In her Millennial world, that possibility is so farfetched Molly won't consider it. She'll find a tower, farmhouse, rural bar, or far-flung gas station with wi-fi to propel her forward, to help her find her way to her destination.

As erroneous as I find my daughter's assurance that she'll discover a signal, I value and celebrate her commitment to that promise. There will be something or someone, somewhere, to deliver her.

Living here, on top of this wooded rise on a dead-end road not much longer than a driveway, I calibrate and celebrate my surroundings with the same self-confidence as my daughter combs for at least one bar on her phone to guide her wherever she's headed. Field and woods and lake and pastures and farms and sunsets and foxes and herons pilot me. The incense of newly-mown grass, its particulates finding their way behind my sunglasses like snowflakes fluttering my eyelids; the succulent taste of bulbous red tomatoes picked that afternoon off the vine; the *rat-a-tat-tat-tat-tat* of a pileated woodpecker at work in a tree above the chicken coop; the rough, leather-like bark of branches a storm's bluster picks off; the ghastly mist on a chilly October morning lifting over the lake's silent surface.

A Map of the Beautiful helps me find where I'm going and reminds me where I've been. I've signal enough to follow its blue and red lines of various thicknesses. My map is beautiful, at least in part, because it is mine. I know that now, finally, at 75-years-old.

The map, naturally, is not as clearly read as it once was. The names of small towns and thread-thin creeks blur. Sometimes I can't distinguish the borders between states and states of mind. Differentiating green and blue herons, even though color and size are dead giveaways, confound me. When hunting for my binoculars, I always find them somewhere else.

It is in the working, the writing, that the Map clarifies, and thus suffices. Each letter tapped out is a finger tracing the journey over the folds. Each letter slides onto the next. And the next.

And the next.

Until the last one leads me home.

Cornwall Village: "A Remembrancer Designedly Dropt"

"A child said, What is the grass?
fetching it to me with full hands....
I guess it is the handkerchief of the Lord,
A scented gift and remembrancer designedly dropt."
Walt Whitman, *Song of Myself*, Section 6

The one square block of Cornwall Village, an hour's drive northwest of Hartford, set above Coltsfoot Valley's long, green meadow, might be God's handkerchief, dropped to remind us what beauty and tranquility can be found in a small rural Connecticut town. Returning fifty-two years after graduating from The Marvelwood School, and writing about it now, I can make that comparison, seeing—and feeling—its halcyon beauty.

Which was nothing like the psychological thunderstorm raging when, at thirteen-years-old, I said goodbye to my mother in Chicago's Union Station five decades ago. Sitting up in a coach seat overnight, all I had to think about was how much

I would miss my luxury Lake Shore Drive apartment with parking attendants, uniformed doormen, part-time laundress, and live-in cook and cat; my friends from the elementary, grade, and middle school I cherished from Junior Kindergarten; weekends exploring the woods and ravines surrounding the private Pullman mansion on rails my grandfather bought when it was retired in 1935, perched above Rock Creek's slow carp and turtle-filled waters outside Plano, Illinois (yes, the tackle box town).

Arriving in New York, I carried my two suitcases through Grand Central Station until a dapper, bespectacled, blue-blazered Mr. Smith from the school made himself known. We vanned north for what seemed like hours before turning south off Route 4 and entered Cornwall Village from where I wouldn't leave until mid-December, for Christmas vacation. After checking in with the M.O.D. (Master of the Day), I was assigned a room in Rumsey Hall, its exterior Greek columns and bold Colonial façade masking its interior rooms with endless ceilings, fissured walls, and splintery wooden floors.

My return to Cornwall more than a half a century later found everything changed and nothing changed.

"Where do you want to go first?" my wife, Tia, asked as she, my daughter Molly, and I turned off Route 4, civilization left behind completely as if entering a magic wardrobe or The Shire. A sunny somnambulance enveloped Molly's Camry like a benign fog. Tia and I had flown from our home in Geneva, Illinois, an hour west of Chicago, where we both taught in parochial secondary schools, to see Molly, a doctoral student in Creative Studies at University of Connecticut. It was mid-July. The trees billowed green and full above us as we crept past where Calhoun House, my junior year dorm, surely stood, although time and memory hid it from me.

"There's a historical society." Tia pointed to a sign in front of a typical Cornwall house. If she'd indicated pterodactyl roadkill, I couldn't have been more disbelieving. An historical society? For Cornwall?

"I need to go to the bathroom," I said, my mantra at 70-years-old. "Let's see if the library's open."

We parked across the street, feeling fairly safe from being ticketed (in my four years as a preppie in town, I never saw a police car or officer). Although closed, the library offered a partial peek into the auditorium where I once played a guard in Shakespeare's Henry IV. The director, most likely an English teacher, encouraged me, for the sake of verisimilitude, to remove my glasses before going onstage, leaving me grasping not only orally when delivering my one or two lines, but visually as well. More successful was the variety show night my freshman roommate Bob Lamb and I did impressions of ABC's Harry Reasoner and Howard K. Smith reporting faux news.

"Maybe we should start at the historical society," Tia suggested, the idea of a toilet inside more an incentive for me than reviewing the past. We walked back through the 85-degree afternoon, umbrellaed from the sun by occasional trees to the air-conditioned house where a young volunteer behind a small desk welcomed us. I told the man I was a Marvelwood graduate, a fact that brought a smile both polite and pitying, as if I'd confessed to him that I'd never had my bunions removed.

The largest display, a wall full of photos, chronologically unfolded the July 10, 1989, tornado that ripped up many of Coltsfoot Valley's Cathedral Pines. Coincidentally, leaving at 1:00 p.m. today, the museum offered a "30th Anniversary Hike in Cathedral Pines." Not that I would have signed on if the group hadn't already departed, but it felt like we'd arrived in town on a holy day everyone else had remembered and prepared for.

Strolling back to the welcome desk, I asked the docent, "Is Rumsey still there?" in the same manner a swimmer might ask a lifeguard, "Is the shark still offshore?"

"No," he said, noticeably sad, which meant he'd never boarded there. "The tornado took off part of Rumsey Hall's roof. In 2010, the village decided to demolish it."

"Thank God!" I blurted, unable to control my ecstasy, turbulent memories still clear, nightmares returning often.

One such recurring dream manifested from a Saturday night after the cafeteria movie and thrilling pulp fiction chapter from "The Spider's Web" (...on speckled black and white film, a fancy 1930's Dodge racing along a dark night road [cut to] a speeding train headed toward certain disaster unless [cut to] The Spider, in close-up, face wrapped in what looks like a black sheet covered with white tic-tac-toe games, can stop it). Returning that night to the dorm, I opened my door, flicked on the light, and saw a rat, seemingly the size of a cougar, scurry across the room, leaving a blond potato chip trail to his escape route, down a radiator pipe's hole. He had bored a hole into the bag beneath which broken golden nuggets pooled. I stuffed the hole with towels and later lay in bed, in the dark, unable to move, unable to sleep, listening for the rat's return, an image that haunted me long after leaving Cornwall.

The next morning, when I told the teacher in charge of my dorm wing, he scoffed, "That's what you get for having food in your room, Holinger."

The single positive attribute Rumsey's age offered was its creaky floors, an alarm that seniors or masters stalked the hall, giving us time to shut up or ditch whatever we were reading instead of solving geometry problems or writing an English paper. Only once was permission to leave our rooms from the 7:20 to 9:50 study hall hours granted, the night we gathered in the building's main hall, bare and echoing, to watch the Fab Four perform before screaming girls on The Ed Sullivan Show in blurry shades of gray.

On the way out, I picked up the museum's free brochures and stopped to read Mark van Doran's "The Little Hills of Cornwall," the poem spelled out on the wall behind the welcome desk. In my journal, written later that day, I critiqued the verse as "trite and silly," but I'd just skimmed the wall rendering. When I Google it now and read it more slowly, its personification still cloys, but my initial review seems reductive.

The poem channels Eliot's cat curling about the house in "Prufrock," or maybe Sandburg's "little cat feet" in "Fog." But one still wonders how the author of this poem could have influenced the likes of Berryman, Ginsberg, Kerouac, and Merton.

As we left the museum and walked back to the car, Tia asked if I wanted to walk around the town's one main block or drive. "Let's drive," I said, unable to repeat one more time those thousands of perambulations from dorm(s) to dining room and classroom buildings under blazing hot suns, harsh cloudbursts, and frigid snowstorms. Occasionally we were sent back to collect forgotten texts or homework during the class day, English teacher Ed Sundt directing profligates, "On your horse!"

Driving leisurely as Dickinson's coach driver Death, we passed the Congregational Church or, as listed in the historical brochure, the United Church of Christ. In that puritanically bare interior, the school gathered on Sunday late afternoons for Vespers, a non-denominational service in which guest speakers tried to keep us from spending the forty-five minutes entertaining ourselves by farting and giggling. The one orator I remember from four years of pew sitting, a prison chaplain, had us at, "I'm not so good with names, but I'm a whizz at numbers."

Next door, or what used to be next door, a flat, unmown, grassy plot was all that marked where Rumsey Hall once stood. Glee filled me as we glided past, as though Tough the Bully had finally gotten his due, or the Wicked Witch of the West had melted into obscurity.

"Do you want to take a picture?" Tia asked.

No, I didn't. Too many pictures remained in my mind: the rat, of course, but also the communal non-draining soapy basement shower stall, the non-partitioned toilets, the bony, uncarpeted floors. Historical significance be damned; this building, like the Confederacy, did not deserve remembrance.

On the afternoon of November 22 of my freshman year, as I rode my bike from Rumsey back to afternoon classes, a passing student called out, "Kennedy's been shot!" As monumental the news was everywhere else, hitting the world like an errant meteor, its impact on Cornwall, sequestered from the world, mattered little. Getting to class on time, getting the homework done, getting through soccer practice—or was it the beginning of hockey season?—took precedence.

We drove past the grassy clearing where a brown path, thin as the tundra hairline trail taken by Jack London's *chechaquo*, cut across to the campus center. To our left, the practice field still stood where our bespectacled, British-born soccer coach once yelled, "It's the SNAP of the knee!" With a population of only ninety-two students, the school encouraged everyone to go out for sports; I spent four years as a fullback toe-kicking goal kicks, my big toe after practices and games bloody and raw.

Another left turn brought us to the barn that once housed our dining room, assembly hall, and miniature basketball court. Today, the museum docent had told us, it was a private residence. Stately brick Calhoun House now held two artists and their studio. In Spring, 1963, Calhoun functioned as dorm, classroom building, and administrative center. My mother and I had sat across the desk from Bob Bodkin, the school's founder and headmaster, who told us he'd take me as long as I went to Maine's Winter Harbor Reading Camp that summer.

I did learn how to read in that rambling seacoast house where bunk beds allowed rooms for four to six other non-readers, and where every morning I'd vomit before breakfast from homesickness. Taught to read actively (skim, read/underline, review), I pass on that wisdom to my high school students today. However, as well as the camp taught me how to read, it didn't make me enjoy reading. That enlightenment came later, at Marvelwood, but not in a classroom.

One day, my roommate, Bob Lamb, reading a novel in a comfy chair he'd brought from home, asked, "Hey, Holinger, how come you never read anything?"

Lamb had a knack for asking impertinent, aggressive questions that suggested there was something wrong with me. I don't know how I answered, but I'm sure his tone pissed me off, so I probably offered up something witty like, "Why do you care?"

"Here," he said, throwing a paperback at me. "Read this."

I looked at the title. *The Arrangement*, by Elia Kazan. I started reading it, and something happened. I became absorbed in the story. I cared about the characters and their world. I was reading satire. I was reading about rebellion from the expected, routine, suburban middle-class life.

If Bob hadn't thrown me that book, I might be rich, but stressed out, might be donning a dark business suit, starchy white-collared shirt and monochrome tie every day, and carrying cost-ratio figures or legal renderings in a monogrammed leather briefcase. Instead, I've spent forty-plus years teaching high school English with a smattering of years as a night-class community college adjunct instructor. When not preparing lesson plans, grading papers, or responding to emails, I'm writing a column for a local paper, facilitating a creative writing group, or writing the occasional essay, poem, or short story.

Winter Harbor's reading skills helped my freshman grades, although not as much as Marvelwood's emphasis on study skills and time management. Assignment planners, proctored study halls, small class sizes, individuated learning, and teachers' close scrutiny of reading and homework assignments all contributed to my success in college (Hartwick), a Master's in English (Washington University), and a doctorate in Creative Writing (University of Illinois at Chicago). Bob Bodkin's dream of taking a kid with unused potential was realized in me, among hundreds of others.

Now, to our right, Coltsfoot Valley looked just as lush and serene as remembered. While attending school, I didn't see it for its Emersonian Transcendental joy, never experienced his "transparent eyeball" at one with forest, meadow, and brook. Instead, my homesick adolescence merely gazed on the idyllic scene apart from it, longing to be somewhere other than where cows grazed and firs swayed. Feeling locked within a rural dystopia, escape for me only over the two major holidays, Christmas and Easter, flying from Bradley Field to O'Hare, I cried every time returning home when an older brother or parent stood waiting for me at Arrivals.

We drove down the narrow valley road where once I pedaled a pre-driven bike bought from a graduating senior, its twisted rear wheel brushing the fender with each revolution. Most off-campus sign-outs wanted to smoke or drink down here, but I was too scared of discovery and expulsion, content to wander as if lost, if only for an hour or two, until curfew called us back.

Returning from the valley, we passed the red clay tennis courts beside Smith House, their nets still in place. After dinner, in the fall and spring, during that golden half-hour between being excused from the dining room until organized study hall (in our dorm rooms or library, depending on behavioral and academic standing), occasionally I'd hit the ball with Lamb or others.

On the courts' far side, hockey players laid out and erected the wood and wire "boards" for the natural-ice rink. Before we had ice, Coach Smith, a non-skater, had us shooting off plywood boards at goalies in pads and sneakers. When snowfall laid a solid base, we signed up for one-hour shifts, hosing it down throughout the night. When we finished, we'd trudge with frozen gloves and glazed boots to Smith House where hot chocolate and cookies waited.

Speaking of Smith House, my sophomore year dorm, its homey, inviting, rooms were a delight after Rumsey. Mrs. Smith's ebullient smile, infectious laugh, and engaging personality occasionally invited us down to her and Mr. Smith's living room after study hall for tea or soda, and some sugary treat.

Late one winter night that year, my roommate woke me returning from his rendezvous with another drinker somewhere in Cornwall's moon shadows. He made it far enough into the room to just miss the end of my bed when throwing up jug wine all over the wall. Whether he didn't want to expose his sin to senior proctors by going to a toilet or couldn't make it there, I never found out.

This same roommate invited a few of us to spend a Holden Caulfield weekend in New York City at his parentless apartment. After a raucous train ride, laughter partnered with Rum Soaked Crooks at Grand Central, we stopped by the Oyster Bar to brandish our fake eighteen-year-old I.D.s. Almost fifteen years younger than Nick Carroway, I got drunk for the first time that night, and ever since have not been able to stomach screwdrivers.

Once past Smith House, the town tour completed, we left Cornwall Village for what, for me, will be the last time. Crossing Route 4, we headed toward West Cornwall on a scenic two-lane with hills, curves, and majestic trees shading our way. Five miles distant, too far for us students to walk, my friends and I rode bikes, panting uphill, whizzing down.

West Cornwall held a dragon's treasure back then, the mountain of gold including candy, chips, dips, and drinks from lemonade bottles to chocolate milk cartons, all unavailable at the one retail outlet near school, the gas station (Sinclair?—I tend to remember a dinosaur on an unlit sign) behind Rumsey, down the hill, past the varsity field. The bagged loot brought back we stored in our rooms; although needing to last until the next trip, a week or more, with our ravenous, gluttonous dorm mates who didn't make the trip cajoling, bullying, and/or paying for our caches, its life span no more than a few days. Dairy and other products needing refrigeration we propped on winter windowsills, often confiscated by seniors, discovered and destroyed (or consumed?) by proctors, stolen by recalcitrant students, or simply lost to wind or careless handling, dropping, exploding one or two stories below.

Today, the tiny town seemed even smaller than when explored as starving adolescents. We crossed the Housatonic on the famous covered bridge and drove that scenic river road toward Marvelwood's new Skiff Mountain campus. When the female GPS navigator led us up a steep, dark, narrow, winding gravel road, we doubted her expertise and began to believe ourselves lost. Suddenly, we mounted a summit, the sky opened, and the new school blossomed around us, the green background lush and inviting, the buildings modern and angular. All three of us laughed, thinking nowhere else in Connecticut could a campus be more sequestered from the world than in Cornwall Village. But, perhaps, this was.

Bob Bodkin's vision may have been hampered by the small town's insularity and housing choices. When seated for morning assembly in metal folding chairs or in hardback wooden chairs at dining room tables, perhaps what I felt back then, if it could have been verbalized, was a lack of coherence, of fitting in, this desolate beauty so radically different from Chicago's Gold Coast that my four years of boarding school seemed an out-of-body experience. A ghosting.

One final anecdote. When dining room seating assignments were posted every week, groans erupted from those sentenced to the headmaster's table. Not only were exquisite table manners expected with the likes of Mr. and Mrs. Bodkin present, but the family style serving, portions were handed out slowly, deliberately, preventing the table's waiter (underclassmen took turns) from going back to the kitchen for seconds (when available) before other tables with less scrupulous manners.

At lunch one day, sitting stiffly and quietly, keeping my elbows off the table and trying not to attract attention, Mrs. Bodkin, model of propriety and conversational acumen, posed a question to the assembled sufferers, fake smiles glued on: "Do you believe in capital punishment?"

A couple of students, probably upperclassmen, mumbled something abstract and non-committal, their answers lost to me now. When no one else spoke, the headmaster's wife turned to me. "Rick, what about you?"

Having no clue what "capital punishment" meant other than it might have something to do with the alphabet taking note of proper nouns, I wavered, dodged, hummed, and hawed until she took mercy on my obvious ignorance and embarrassment and picked her next victim.

Let that moment serve as a metonymy for my years at Marvelwood (1963-7). I wasn't ready for it, but I was better off for it. Blindsided by the loneliness of being a long-distant student, I nevertheless left four years later knowing more about myself than the academic curricula. The greatest gift the school offered, Edwin Sundt, my freshman and junior year English teacher, encouraged my writing, especially by selecting me as co-editor of *Marvelit*, the Marvelwood literary magazine. I still have faded carbon copies of my feeble attempts at fiction and poetry that slowly disappear, thankfully, with every passing year.

The John Updike write-for-a-living plan didn't pan out for me, but I published a couple of innovative short fiction chapbooks, a book of poetry, and a collection of my local newspaper columns in which I continually throw my wife and children under the bus. Even though written over the next half century, these books surely began in some fashion the day that school van, carrying a scared, homesick, lonely kid from Chicago first turned south off Route 4 and entered for the first time the village that would be his home for the next four years.

And, in many ways, his home for the next fifty-two.

Manure Dreams

My two oldest brothers slog back from the barns manure tired, smelling of pigsty sludge and tractor exhaust. Straw from the bales they've pitched sticks to sleeve-rolled, sweat-stained t-shirts and dusty denim, pantlegs folded twice like the bikers in black-and-white films. Corn dust salts Brad's curly brown hair and Langston's light blond hair. Their thin faces look not so much dirty as clouded, their expressions the tone of the sky before a downpour. In 1960, they are fifteen and seventeen respectively.

Before they go inside the train car, they take off their engineer (or motorcycle) boots, what they call shitkickers when adults are not around. Our mother ordered them from the telephone-book-thick, thin-paged Sears, Roebuck & Co. catalogue. My next eldest brother, Patrick, and I, also own shitkickers, but while we try to ornament ours as elegantly as Brad and Langston, we can only envy their mud, muck, and pea-sized gravel from filled potholes on the quarter mile of asphalt drive laid twenty years ago connecting farm outbuildings barns to the Pullman, our summer residence.

The boots stand side-by-side next to cement stairs leading up to the *Constitution*'s back door. In white athletic socks, Brad and Langston go through the metallic screen door, its bottom screeching across worn, black tiles, through the small entry where a second refrigerator holds Cokes, ginger ales, and frozen chicken potpies, past the thick, heavy door, hooked open, into the galley.

Or maybe with all its upgrades, today it's a kitchen: built-in dishwasher and electric stove, freestanding refrigerator, white metal cabinets, and gray Formica countertops. Where an upper berth used to swing down at night for a crew member, one lone recessed nightlight hints at the berth's removal, in its place an aluminum popcorn popper and shiny, mirrored toaster. Not all is lost: a brown-handled axe stands erect behind elongated, framed glass, a crack running down its length.

Another glassed-in box, barely big enough for a pair of women's flats, attaches above a white wooden table the size of a full-breakfast tray. Inside, tiny brass arrows indicate the source of service requested by passengers when pushing a button in staterooms A, B, C, or D, rear observation lounge, or dining room, prompting the gold arrow to swing from its sideways position upward, pointing to the inscribed destination desiring attention.

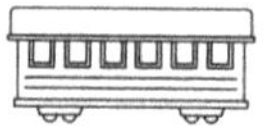

Langston stakes out the best of the four staterooms, A, and Brad the second best, D, both with full-size mattress beds that permanently replaced couches once facing each other. My grandfather added external bathrooms by cutting holes in the side of the car and building spaces large enough for a small sink, toilet, and walk-in shower—with barely enough room to towel off. A and D are no larger than a tiny fourth bedroom in a traditional colonial home, but each fits a heavy set of dark wooden drawers topped with felt and glass, above which a square, framed mirror reflects the built-in closet next to the door stamped with a gold-stenciled "A." Above, two small Tiffany windows open with what looks like a wood-handled harpoon, its metal hook catching and pulling down a centered O ring. The same type of stick and claw mechanism can pull out and unroll over the bed a canvas cover protecting the sleeper from the locomotive's soot sweeping in the windows.

Our parents sleep in the only truly comfortable bedroom, off a small living room with fireplace, an addition added to the exterior of the train car.

Because seniority counts in our family, my next older brother, Patrick, and I sleep in staterooms B and C with pulldown berths and, beneath, facing couches made into beds. Each room is outfitted with a Pullman green felt-padded seat cover that opens to a toilet, its copper handle pulled up to flush away the waste with swishing water. Perched above a tiny white porcelain sink that ran water with foot pedals is a built-in mirrored wooden cabinet barely large enough for toothpaste and toothbrushes. A nearly full-length mirror fills most of the wooden door that separates each stateroom, at least two or three shattering over the years with angry slamming.

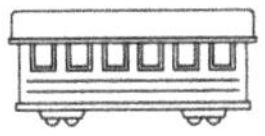

According to a local 1935 newspaper article, to transport the *Constitution* half a mile from the main tracks slicing through Plano (fifty miles southwest of Chicago) to a bluff overlooking Big Rock Creek, Langston, Sr., my mother's father, hired William Tracy of Aurora, a professional mover, to remove the undercarriage and lift the car onto the backs of two tractor trailer trucks. After winding down the hill behind where, in seventeen years, the first plastic Plano tackle box would be molded, the trucks turtled through spring's floodplain where soft, moist earth stopped them for so many days my grandfather believed he'd have to leave his car there, vulnerable to water that could rise more than a dozen feet. He was saved by the hired farmer whose barns and fields Langston, Sr. also bought, the massive tractors pulling the trucks free of the muck, allowing them to finish hauling their payload up the hill.

Ready for the rails in 1906, one of a metallic pack of *Mansions on Wheels* (as Lucius Beebe titled his 1959 book), the *Constitution*, originally framed in wood, was remodeled with steel vestibules the following year. Its interior, with inlaid wooden craftsmanship and Tiffany windows and wall lamps, could sleep twelve to fourteen, leased for a daily rate of $75.00, or $50.00 for two or more days. According to railroad historian Wayne Johnston, the charter came with a cook and two attendants. In addition to the pianist, composer, and prime minister of Poland after WWI, Ignace Paderewski, two United States presidents, Coolidge and Harding, rode it, their early 20th century's Air Force One.

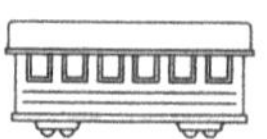

In summer and on weekends, our father, an internationally renowned otolaryngologist, drives the two-hour trip (before expressways) to the Pullman. On Saturday nights, he takes the family to the Friendly Tap on Plano's Main Street for "a steak." I never know what other options the bar offers because we never see a menu, our only choice between a New York strip and ribeye. Dad has a beer with dinner, my mother a vodka on the rocks.

After dinner, if something good is playing around the corner at the Plano Theater, we catch a movie like *Cape Fear*, the original, with Gregory Peck and Robert Mitchum, that has me replaying with horror for years the scenes where Mitchum dispatches the lookouts.

Or we go back to the train car and gather in the sunroom, a window-walled, three-season room perched over the bluff, its brick fireplace rivaling Charles Foster Kane's marble monstrosity at Xanadu. In winter, built-in side fans blow barely enough warm air into the room to accommodate the watching on a black and white console TV's iconic Saturday night lineup, *Gunsmoke, Have Gun, Will Travel*, and *Perry Mason*.

On Sundays, Langston and Brad do not walk up to the barns to work. Instead, my father directs us in jobs he wants done for free. In fall, we rake leaves down the long, steep bank into the creek, so spring irises could grow. The four of us tramp behind my father through the woods until finding a dead or fallen tree to saw up or chop down, followed by propping the trunk and largest branches on sawhorses we use to lop off logs the length of the two-man saw we take turns pushing and pulling. Even with gloves on, splinters spear our hands, some large enough to pull out clean with fingernails.

In early winter, on the garage windows, we change out lighter screens for heavy, cobwebbed storms. In mid-spring, when very young, we mow lawns with a hand-pushed, squeaking, circular blade mower, only years later graduating to a pull-cord push gasoline rotary mower.

Across the crumbling driveway, the distance of an outfielder's throw to home plate west of the train car, cattle range behind a five-foot fence topped with barbed wire. A decade later, in the late 60s or early 70s, they no longer graze there, corralled in barns and pens, less chance of breaking a leg when spooked or eating anything not charitable to the prices at meat markets.

But before the fence comes down and the field develops into a manicured softball diamond surrounded by woods and cornfield, its tall grasses cut with a large rotary mower pulled by a John Deere tractor, we climb over the barrier and shoo the skittish, slow-moving black and brown-and-white cattle, their coarse furry coats caked with dried dung, out of the "infield" and "outfield" to play a game. Inevitably, rounding the bases (extra mitts, sweatshirts, or windfallen branches), we step in a cow pie, its yellow interior squeezing through its potpie crust, the horror of the occasion and resulting odor squelching jubilation or fears of finding ourselves "safe" or "out."

When not directing us in chores, my father putters. He builds birdhouses for which we're occasionally roped into screwing in a screw, sawing a side or roof, or pounding in a nail. In spring, he hangs them on branches, and, in fall, he takes them down, unscrews the floors, and cleans out the nesting. He erects a purple martin house at the edge of the cornfield in sight of the train car, its lighthouse height attracting nothing but housebreakers.

If not content with the bird population near the train car, he urges us to go on a walk through the floodplain. Starting down the hill on the asphalt road already breaking into shards, we cross the wooden bridge over the runoff creek toward hundreds of acres of corn and soy fields half a mile away, and cross over the mill race where a rusting wheel once raised and lowered a blade to regulate water flow north a quarter mile to the mill, later renovated as Plano's Town Hall. Climbing over the wooden gate beside the fence keeping cattle from wandering up the hill, we stop at the cement dam halting not water but cattle from walking upriver, its smooth overflow sloping down to a flat twelve-foot-long shelf eventually falling into the sand and pebble riverbed. When swimming there, we wear cutoff jeans and worn-out t-shirts, sidestepping carefully along the slippery top, water running over our worst sneakers, then sit down and push off, sliding down on our butts, the water splashing up when stopped at the bottom, our ragged swimwear green stained from long, sinewy seaweed.

Past the dam, we weave through the woods, the road no more than a grass and gravel path. Once part of a golf course, the first tee perched on top of the hill west of the mill, the floodplain could be taken in from one end to the other clearly as an Arizona desert. Hearing familiar bird calls, Dad looks up and spots the target immediately, naming it and chirping back. I never see what he sees. Whether it's my Buddy Holly-thick glasses or just my displeasure with the sport of looking for nondescript birds, the winged felons evade my sight. Where my father and brothers spot songbirds and *rat-a-tat-tatting* woodpeckers, I find only a thick, green morass of impenetrable leaves in summer, and naked, anorexic black limbs in winter.

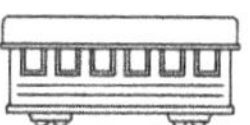

Unlike my father, my mother, Juniper, dislikes it here. Born and raised on Chicago's Gold Coast in a condo overlooking Lake Shore Drive and the lake, she is accustomed to Society: lunch and bridge at the Women's Athletic Club ("WAC"); dinner at the Casino (not a gambling joint, but the city's most prestigious private club, where teenage cotillions are held for young women "coming out," or "debuting"); swimming and tennis at the Saddle and Cycle Club. She serves as Junior League president and oversees the secretaries at my father's Michigan Avenue medical office, often bringing to the dinner table complaints of how the women are not living up to her expectations.

But it's not bugs, bats, or bedlam that keeps my mother from loving the place that to the men in the family is a halcyon sanctuary from city, school, and doctors' appointments. Yes, she does have a phobia of snakes, and occasionally the barn cat we brought back from northern Wisconsin returns from hunting in the woods to show off a squirming garter or pine snake in his mouth. Rather, her mother and father divorced in their sixties, Langston having taken up with a much younger woman we four sons knew as "Aunt Lucille." Apparently, Langston used the train car for his (somewhat) surreptitious rendezvous with Lucille, tainting for my mother the rustic charm of the *Constitution* and its surrounding oaks, maples, and poplars; its deer, raccoon, and squirrels; and its iris, daffodils, and bluebells. What should have been a place of inclusion and family love, for her became a place of division and lust.

During those long summer weeks when Langston and Brad kick stones up to the barns where they earn a man's hourly wage—or at least a teenager's—riding horses rounding up cattle feeding on floodplain grasses, slopping out pig and sheep pens, throwing haybales, and other farm chores, Patrick and I work less glamorous jobs. Armed with thistle sticks (snake forked-tongue blades on the end of heavy, five-foot long wooden poles) and spades (a shovel with a supposedly sharpened blade and point), with the promise from our father half a penny for each thistle's roots unearthed (not just broken off to grow again), we head down to the floodplain.

At whatever stage the thistle grows, its strongest personality trait is its obstinacy, from its early numerous hairy, spiked, emerald leaves spreading over pale green grass, to a fully developed, three-to-five-foot thick, spiked, and feathery mint green stem protected by multiple daggered leaves topped off with an evil spiked bolus (reminding one of a knight's vicious "morning star flail") sprouting a lovely violet head of hair the Muppets' Beaker would envy. A bull thistle's roots are strong, deep, and stubborn.

Thistle sticks work only on the few nascent plants not yet grounded some feet below. The spades need to either cut through roots seemingly thick as car pistons or dig so far out from the stem that the blade slips in more easily, but so much dirt comes up with the thistle that heaving up and turning over the load becomes a sweat-laden, arduous task. Either method makes the exercise tiring and monotonous.

Sure, the feeding cattle eat better for our labor, the point of the endeavor, but when we finally drag ourselves back uphill, my hands have blistered through leather gloves, my glasses are smeared with sweat, and the soles of my shitkickers are caked yellow from stepping on the thousands of sunbaked, crusted cow pies, just as my Keds had been when worn for softball. Only a jet stream hose nozzle will clean the creamy custard filling.

My brothers and I pass rites of passage. When each of us turn twelve, my father takes us in turn to Plano's hardware store where we pick out a B-B gun and our first cardboard tube of copper B-Bs. We shoot trees, rocks, and other enemies.

When turning sixteen, we go with him to Chicago downtown's VL&A (Abercrombie and Fitch), where we pick out our style of .22 rifle and a box of short rifle bullets. Langston chooses a bolt-action with clip; Brad a pump; Patrick a curved lever action; and I the classic straight lever action of the iconic Winchester 73. We take our rifles to the gravel pit and shoot cans and crudely drawn targets. From the bank beside the train car, we fire downhill into the creek at mud-wallowing carp as if we can hurt them, never once raising one to the surface, surely not smart enough to figure in refraction, their only response a flashbulb spark of a sideways thrust through stirred-up bottom mud.

To the west and south of the *Constitution*, a runoff creek, usually dry, its sandy bottom and tangled-root banks making a better fort or trench than a moat, slices along the bottom of a woody ravine barb-wired with curled thorn bushes that can stab through denim. I spend hours climbing, exploring, and playing out scenarios while packing my tan Fanner 50 belt, holster, and metal silver pistol.

Inevitably, a gang of outlaws have escaped, and I, the brave, lone, independent lawman, go in search of the culprits. Always outnumbered, always invincible, I might get wounded (never in my shootin' arm), even get shot off my horse (I can do a mean imitation of a galloping and walking stallion), but only to heighten suspense, inflate dramatic tension, and prepare for satisfying closure. Imagined characters and unfolding narratives are to me as palpable as the low stumps I trip over; years later, in graduate school, I understand Marianne Moore's definition of poetry: "imaginary gardens with real toads."

Before I began writing poetry and short stories, I am playing them.

I am playing the *Constitution*, its *click-clacking* back-and-forth motion charging along invisible tracks, hauling historic freight.

I am playing Big Rock Creek, its sunning mud turtles with shells larger than extra-large pizzas, and underwater snapping turtles sitting still as rocks, mouths open, tongues wriggling like seductive worms enticing smallmouth bass inside jaws set to crush their catch.

I am playing the woods, once pristine and uncluttered, easy to see deer through, over the decades obscured by invasive honeysuckle, autumn olive, oriental bittersweet, buckthorn, garlic mustard, and multiflora rose, some strangling trees with noose-thick vines or pushing out wildflowers and saplings with broad, shady stems.

And I am playing at how to write, the hikes, the pretense, the waters, the woods, the animals, and the traditions all later prompts, essential minutiae every early childhood holds, whatever cityscape, mountainscape, or farmscape inhabited. They are the past from which writers make something more than memories.

They are the manure caked on one's shitkickers.

Growing Up Gold Coast

We didn't have to traffic to the lake. We lived twelve stories above it, on Lake Shore Drive's Gold Coast. Marshall Field and Kemper of Kemper Insurance lived in the same building. Once I rode the elevator down with opera singer Pavarotti. He grumbled because he had to wait for more than a minute after he pushed the DOWN button for the elevator to rescue him.

In our home, allowance appeared regularly as silver flatware. Cookies always filled the tin, and Cokes were always cold. Manners were enforced with European formality. There were enough siblings for a tennis team. We called for our cars on a house phone a garage man picked up and drove from the indoor parking lot to the front door. My brothers and I trick-or-treated up and down in an elevator, never leaving the building. Having a Swiss and English heritage and being confirmed Midwestern Presbyterians neutralized us, made us a majority of the majority. We grew into bodies that functioned well enough for sports, and our looks, if not handsome with glasses and a chubby face, were upper-middle-class and as clean cut as the lives we were taught to lead.

As soon as we could walk, we were taken to Symphony Hall, to a velvet-cushioned chairs in a box just above the percussion section. We held our ears. The black suits we wore, 100-percent wool, prickled the backs of our legs for two hours.

When dexterous enough, we took piano lessons on our grandmother's grand. We survived two piano teachers, the first an immense Margarette Rutherford woman of fifty who left little room on the bench for us. The second, a perfectly coiffed man with white hair in his forties whose nails clicked over the ivory keys when he played. We went through the motions, playing the pieces chosen for us; in growing up Gold Coast, there was no choosing of masters.

"That sounded delightful, dear," mother would encourage after our fifteen minutes of practice was up. "I like that piece particularly. So does your father." Our father cared about music as discipline.

"Particularly well," he would add.

Our Gold Coast building had a doorman to carry luggage, open doors, and deliver polite good mornings, afternoons, and nights, and an elevator man who stood like a jet pilot next to his machine, ready to take it up. Every so often we would have to wait a moment outside the revolving doors for a janitor dressed in gray to finish polishing the brass plates where hands pushed. Glass chandeliers hung in the lobby, and when the sun shone in, hundreds of rainbows rained onto deep leather chairs facing each other. Between them, a turn-of-the-century walnut table stood on a Persian rug spread over black and white marble squares. In addition to elegance, the surroundings advanced a maturity and character of a class still convinced of its place in society.

In our incipient years at The Latin School of Chicago, we handed out chocolate and wore watches our father brought back from Switzerland. We competed for the tallest arrangement of letter blocks, the smoothest reading from *Dick and Jane*, the steadiest penmanship. We impressed girls with rude talk we would not use at home. Teachers elongated our nicknames into formal monikers.

Education lengthened our lives.

We played after school in Lincoln Park, the rich people's park, the statue of a seated Vardeman Green Black looking down Astor Street as we set up football boundaries with Abercrombie plaids, Capper & Capper downs, Brooks' cashmeres. We kicked off with a Duke from Mage's and returned it with footing from Morsan's. We broke eyeglasses from the House of Vision and ripped blue jeans from Field's.

We learned conventions early. Saturday night, instead of watching *Gunsmoke*, we were driven to dancing school at the Fortnightly Club where we learned, from a dancing instructor with castanets and whiskey breath, how to foxtrot and jitterbug on a floor waxed for weddings. We learned when, how, and why to ask for a dance: politely, with a smattering of disdain, at the beginning of a number, because there will always be competition for partners.

There were country homes to which we escaped.

On weekends, near a farm owned by our grandfather and farmed by a professional farmer, we spent time in a house on a bluff overlooking a creek and forest floodplain where we learned about birds and woodchucks. But we didn't discover the woods on our own; our days were designed, our walks plotted, our play controlled by our father to nailing bird houses, raking leaves, sawing and splitting logs. Nature was ordered for us in western Illinois.

For a month in the summer we headed north to the cool of Wisconsin where in a cabin on a mile-long lake we dismissed and forgot city and school life. The North Woods insulated us, nothing meaner than a snapping turtle permitted on The Club's grounds. We played with children who shared our age, our morality, our convictions, our color. No one contested; no one risked; no one cried. The Club carried us up to and into another school year on fairies' wings.

Our parents did not make the Social Register. After school, invited to our friends' apartments, we buried our jealousy when shown their parents' names in fine black print on thick ivory pages. We wondered what ours had done, or not done, to warrant exclusion. From our vantage point, our parents looked acceptable: an internationally famous surgeon for a father; a *grande dame* for a mother who entertained with elegance and charm, volunteered at hospitals, served as President of the Junior League, and was a member of the Colonial Dames. They had four boys born two years apart; a live-in cook; a nanny; a cat; voted and acted Republican, financially and spiritually.

Puberty arrived. Peers began throwing parties in their homes on Friday and Saturday nights. We danced to The Twist, drank Cokes, ate Fritos, and played the WLS-AM top forty. We could feel parents in the next room. Precious, breakable lamps disappeared, and the rug was covered with plastic. When someone suggested spin-the-bottle, cowards threatened to leave. The girls did not object, and some gathered in a circle. When someone threw an empty Coke bottle into the circle, another doctor's son said it was time for him to go, so we said, "We're leaving, too," faithful to our principles and parents. We learned on the Gold Coast not to risk what we did not comprehend.

Our parents sent us to camp farther north than The Club where we mastered our competitive spirit in swimming races, bow and arrow competitions, wrestling matches, and steeple chases. For those eight weeks, we were homesick. What we did not realize was that our parents had sent us there to give them a break from us, and to expose us to life away from the Gold Coast in preparation and to help us adapt more easily when sent to an Eastern boarding school. Camp was an eight-week training course in what it would feel like freed from what was safe and secure.

Because adolescence on the Gold Coast meant leaving it. Parents did not want menstrual daughters and aggressive males to contend with. We boarded in dormitories with a schoolmaster for every twenty of us. We learned regulation, organization, confiscation. Our lives narrowed to paths of expectations, and although in classrooms we thought we were accumulating something new, we truly learned how to forget. The beauty of the New England campus, set in the Berkshires' Cathedral pines, was lost on us; we did not see them until years later, returning for Alumni Day.

Home for vacations, we watched debutantes debut, coming out like confident groundhogs in spring. They flowed like champagne, in and out of dresses, dances, ballrooms, and love. They settled only long enough to ready themselves for the next night's or season's parties and for viewing by the people at the Saddle & Cycle, Indian Hill, or Onwentsia. After a few years, we began to realize all of us had grown up Gold Coast, and without the mystery of the new, the splendor of the evenings—the tuxedoes, the gowns, the pocketed Jim Beam—disappointed. When summer and Christmas vacations ended, we all had somewhere else to be, and someone else to be with, but nowhere or no one anyone wanted.

Once in college, again far away, most of us outgrew the Gold Coast forever, while some of us grew into it farther than ever. However, like recalling the stumbling attempt of our first kisses, we could not leave it out of our lives as much as we may have tried. It mattered little where we lived, New Haven, St. Louis, Gallup, Seoul; we visited the Gold Coast every day with every decision, with every emotion, and with every person we sought to get to know.

The Gold Coast grew up with us.

Acknowledgements

Great appreciation to these literary journals and their editors for including my creative nonfiction pieces among their pages. Works are listed in the order they appear in this book.

Catamaran: "Receptions: Poetry, The White House, and the Hostage Trees"
Chicago Quarterly Review:" An Encounter on Brookside Pond"
Cimarron Review: "Blowing Toward Winfield"
Cutleaf: "Manure Dreams"
Hobart: "The Foreign Zoo: Tour(s)ing in Place"
Illinois English Bulletin: "Arguing *the Scarlet Letter*'s Demise"
JMWW: "K of C"
Madville Publishing: "Being Home" (anthology): "Cornwall Village: A Remembrancer Designedly Dropt"
Modern Images: "Growing Up Gold Coast"
149 Review: "Good Graces"
Rockford Review: "It's My Novel! It's My Thesis! It's My Novel AND My Thesis!"
South Dakota Review: "A Focus of Enhancement"
Thread: "The Art of Passivity" (A Notable Essay in *The Best American Essays 2018*)

About the Author

Rick Holinger grew up overlooking Lake Michigan on Chicago's Gold Coast but soon left that privileged lifestyle for the life of a high school teacher living in the western 'burbs with his artist wife, Tia (who also taught secondary school), and two children, Jay and Molly, now grown. He'd wake up early and write for an hour or two before his first class, leading to poems, stories, and essays eventually finding homes in *The Southern Review, Boulevard, Cimarron Review, Hobart, North American Review, The Iowa Review, Western Humanities Review, Witness, Chicago Quarterly Review, Chautauqua,* and elsewhere.

Books started sprouting up, including a collection of newspaper columns, *Kangaroo Rabbits and Galvanized Fences,* about which David Hamilton, Editor Emeritus of *The Iowa Review,* writes, Holinger "uses language well, has all sorts of inventive phrasing." About *North of Crivitz,* poetry of the upper Midwest, former Illinois Poet Laureate Kevin Stein notes, "Within these lines one hears Emerson and Frost wrestling in verdant woods."

Not Everybody's Nice, winner of the 2012 Split Oak Press Flash Prose Contest, C. Michael Curtis, former Fiction Editor of *The Atlantic Monthly,* describes as "shrewd glimpses of the human landscape make diverting and surprisingly satisfying reading." A forthcoming short fiction collection, published by Main Street Rag Publications, *Unimaginable Things: Stories*, includes fictions first published in *ACM, The Iowa Review, New Flash Fiction Review, Southern Indiana Review, Witness,* and others.

Holinger's work has been nominated seven times for a Pushcart Prize and two-times for Best of the Net. His story, "Mars," appears in *Best Microfiction 2025* and was nominated for *Best Small Fictions 2025*. He holds a Ph.D. in Creative Writing from The University of Illinois at Chicago, and a Master's degree in English from Washington University, St. Louis. He and Tia live in rural northern Illinois above a small lake where fox, deer, bald eagles, blue herons, redtail hawks, sandhill cranes, and other visions occasionally pass by.

FUN FACT
Choeofpleirn is a word James P. Cooper invented
by combining the letters of
our surnames alternately.
It's pronounced, "chuf-plern"
and loosely means
"the chief place of rest."
We hope you found the literature herein
restful and rejuvenating.
Choeofpleirn Press
A 501(c)3 nonprofit

Choeofpleirn Press
A Kansas private
literary press
www.choeofpleirnpress.com
A 501(3)(c) company

www.choeofpleirnpress.com
choeofpleirnpress@gmail.com

2026